PSYCHIC EMPATH

IMPROVE YOUR PSYCHIC DEVELOPMENT AND CULTIVATE YOUR INNER TALENT. LEARN HOW TO CONNECT WITH YOUR SPIRIT, ABSORB UNIVERSAL ENERGY AND RADIATE POSITIVITY. DISCOVER ALL EMPATH SECRETS

AURORA SULLIVAN & JORDY LUNA

ISBN: 9798665553009

Table of Contents

Introduction

Empaths are hypersensitive individuals with high levels of understanding and compassion for the emotions of other people. They connect with others in a deeper sense and are often known to actually "feel" their emotions.

However, many born empaths are not aware of this fact. They believe that what is happening to them is normal and simply accepted the fact that they are sensitive.

The world is full of empaths. People label them as sensitive. Most of them are artists, singers, or writers. Because of their sensitivity, empaths become poets in motion. They are also very interested in different cultures and view them with a wider perspective.

They are everywhere. They could be anyone among your family, colleagues, peers, friends, or workmates.

Empaths are the world's greatest listeners. Most often, they are the thinkers, the learners, or the problem solvers. Their deep comprehension and understanding of things make them the "wind beneath the wings" of people in their life. For empaths, every problem has an answer and they are always ready to look for one.

Venturing to the far corners of the planet throughout the previous three decades so as to pass on the message of yoga, and find that yoga has impacted the course of human reasoning colossally. At first obviously, there was some uncertainty about it, the same number of individuals imagined that yoga was a sort of religion, black magic or mystery. This especially happened in light of the fact that man accepted issue was a definitive point in the development of nature. The materialistic world didn't comprehend yoga for quite a while, yet as the men of science plunged profound into the secrets of issue, they came to comprehend and understand that issue was not a definitive in the advancement of nature.

In the event that that is so for one type of issue, it applies to each type of issue. This outer experience, the discernment you have through your faculties, is a result of issue. Indeed, even your musings, sentiments, feelings and insights are results of issue. Accordingly, they can't be total and last. This implies there must be another domain of experience. What's more, if there is another domain of experience, it must be conceivable to rise above the current impediments of the psyche.

The brain is likewise matter; it is certainly not soul. So, the brain can likewise be changed and made to advance. Individuals have started to acknowledge and encounter this over the most recent couple of decades. Also, as I would see it, this denotes the finish of one period and the start of another. For the individuals who know about science and the idea of issue, it isn't hard to see precisely what internal experience is.

An internal encounter is simply the appearance of a more profound degree of oneself. Dream, obviously, is an encounter.

Your fantasies might be schizophrenic yet that is your very own declaration self. Thought is additionally an idea or articulation of your own self. A bit of music is a statement of yourself, regardless of whether you form it or simply appreciate it. An artistic creation or figure is an idea of yourself whether you make it or simply respect it. That implies the outside world is an indication of your internal experience. What's more, you can improve this experience to any degree. You can likewise realize disintegration of this experience. When everything is miserable outside, that is your experience of yourself, and if everything is delightful outside, that is additionally your experience of yourself.

1

Developing Psychic Abilities

Get started on the road to feeling empowered and confident in yourself! Remember, even the most experienced or naturally gifted psychics didn't start their journey with complete confidence and power; they had to practice often to gradually increase their abilities. The key is to believe in yourself and stay relaxed. Trust in your ability and intuition, even though, if you've been raised to ignore it, it may feel silly at first. Keep noticing subtle things you sense. Additionally, keep in mind that you should keep practice sessions relatively short, no more than an hour, as longer sessions are unnecessarily draining and exhausting, and you can't be expected to keep your focus that long. Once you've lost your focus, concentration, and grounding, any practice you attempt will be ineffective.

One great technique is writing down potential psychic messages. Try keeping a journal of what you think may be clairvoyant, audient, sentient or cognizant premonitions. Keep track of these recordings and see if anything ever becomes of them – if they're relevant at all. This is an excellent technique for beginners because you can sort out the random bits and pieces from actual psychic messages, and you can start to piece together what a prediction or premonition actually feels like. It may help you to write down how you felt beside each potential message as well.

This can't be reiterated enough. Practice every day. This may sound daunting, but if you keep it up, pretty soon it will come naturally, and you won't even notice you're doing it. Now, if you miss a day or two or more for whatever reason (illness, feeling emotionally drained, etc.), don't worry! Just pick up where you left off and keep testing different techniques and tools. It's not something to panic about if you haven't practiced in a while, you won't lose "the gift" as we all have it, just as your muscles won't deteriorate if you don't go to the gym for a while. This is just to tell you the best and most effective ways of developing your gift's power.

Another highly effective tool is Meditation. We'll go over it more thoroughly in this part, but we'll touch on it now as it is one of the main tools and techniques for developing your psychic intuition.

If you're practicing daily, try incorporating ten to twenty-minute meditation sessions into your daily routine before you try to interpret anything. This will clear out any emotional blockages, thoughts, worries, or distractions you may have both relevant to psychic practice or about your daily life. It also connects you to a higher plane where your spirit guide(s) and psychic energy reside. Connecting with your spirit guide(s) during meditation will also help answer any questions you may have, as they will help you. Meditation empties the mind to help you focus on the spiritual task at hand. For more information on meditation, meditation techniques and spirit guides.

Psychometry is also a really easy technique to try. The word may sound complicated, but all it means is reading the energy of an object. Just pick something up that has some meaning you know, like a family heirloom to start, and focus on the energy coming off of it. Clear your mind and see what comes up. Don't force any images, just let them flow. Once you've practiced like this a few times, try transitioning to an object you don't know the history and meaning of. Go to a thrift store and buy an old silver knick-knack or item of jewelry. Or you can ask a friend to lend you an important item of theirs or their family's without telling you the history and meaning behind it. This way, it's likely to be more effective as you can do the reading in front of your friend, telling them what images, words or feelings come up, and they can tell you whether they have any relevance or accuracy.

Notice certain symbols that reoccur in your premonitions. If you've done any preliminary research on prophecies or predictions, you'll probably have stumbled across some sort of symbol guide —for example, things like red means love, 13 means bad luck, green means wealth, etc. However, what you should know is that there are no universals! Symbols are different for everyone. Tied to the journal idea is the idea to try and keep tabs on what certain images, colors, or numbers tend to symbolize for you.

If possible, surround yourself with like-minded people, such as other psychics or people on the same spiritual path as you. If you find people on the same vibrational level, your energy will rise, and this will help you thrive spiritually. Thus, growing your psychic ability. It's also nice to have positive reinforcement from your peers. If you don't know anyone in your life with a similar idea of spirituality, try finding some online. Different groups or forums on social media can be just as helpful as face-to-face advice and conversation. You can even look up if there are any local groups where you live that you can join and take part in. Try looking for a group with a mix of experienced and beginner psychics. That way, you can get advice and ask questions of the more experienced members while not feeling too intimidated as you have other beginners to practice and compare notes with. Whether online or in your life, it's important to have positive support from like-minded people

Spending time in nature is also a stress reliever to help open your mind. Some of this may just sound like basic life advice that doesn't have much to do with psychic powers, but it's impossible to grow as a psychic if you are stressed and emotionally/energetically blocked. Nature is our roots. Nature was here before us, and it will remain here long after we pass. Walk around and realize that, despite all your worries, the trees will still stand steady. The wind will still blow. The world will not stop. Take in the peace and the ancient energy of nature and let that energy soothe and empty your mind. As discussed, an empty mind is the best way to start a psychic reading.

Ask questions of the universe frequently. Whether you're walking down the sidewalk and are wondering whether you should change careers, or you're relaxing in the bath, wondering if your relationship is working out? No matter where you are and what you're wondering, try to become aware of this and consciously ask the universe for advice. Take it out of the wondering state and purposefully ask the universe, what do I do? How do I figure this out? Get specific. You may not get an immediate answer, but if you wait, a day, a week, maybe a few weeks, the answer will likely deliver itself to you. You need only ask.

If you've been trying these techniques and feel like you're stuck with what to do next, just repeat, repeat, repeat, practice, practice, and practice. The path to developing your psychic powers is different for everyone, but the universal is to remain confident and focused. If there's one technique that feels like it works for you more than the others, focus on that one — whatever is working best to grow your powers.

Next, we will discuss some important tools psychics sometimes choose to use: tarot, crystal ball scrying, palmistry, and tea leaf reading. These are all forms of divination, a way of telling the future. There are other physical tools and methods that psychics can use but let's start with these four. You will likely prefer one over the others or find a certain method comes much more naturally and is easier for you, providing you with more accurate readings. Don't feel pressure to master all of these; they are just possible methods you can use as a psychic.

If you've ever heard of tarot cards, you may have heard that you can't buy your own deck; one has to be gifted to you. This is a myth. You can pick out and buy your own deck, and it won't change anything. When choosing a deck, try and connect with it – its energy has to click with yours. If the artwork really stands out to you, this is also a good sign that it's your deck. Once you have selected your deck, don't try and do any readings right away. You have to spiritually "break it in", so to speak. One way of doing this is taking each card out one by one, and passing it over smoke. This will cleanse its energy. Then, shuffle through the deck and examine each individual card, taking in any feelings the artwork may evoke. Go for a walk with your deck, sleep with it next to your pillow. It's important to intertwine your energies so that the deck is familiar with you and you with it. When you're just starting, you can do readings for yourself, and then maybe ask a friend if you can practice with them. When doing a reading, you can find a spread you like (for example three cards: one for past, one for present and one for future) and while shuffling/before spreading them out, ask the card a question. It can't be a yes or no question because there aren't yes or no cards. However, it can be as vague or specific as you like. If you are doing a reading for someone else, they may want to keep their question private, but let them know that this may make interpreting the message of the cards slightly more difficult. If you are reading for someone else, lay the deck in front of them and ask them to cut the deck into three piles, then choose the top card from each pile (this is one example of a basic spread. If there is another way you feel you want them to draw the cards, or if you want to draw for them, then go for it, there are many different techniques). When each card is flipped over revealing the artwork, check to see if any of them are upside down (decide first which way will be the right way up, facing you or facing them).

2

How Unleash Your Psychic Powers

Think of yourself as a channel for energy to flow into and fill your body. As a receiver for energy, you must put aside your worries, ego, and thoughts. Think of yourself as a mere hollow capsule. You are an open doorway, a place for the energy in the universe to flow through. You will have an easier time achieving a relaxing, peaceful state if you start each meditation with these beliefs.

Leave thoughts of earthly concerns behind when you enter your holy place. You are no longer on Earth. You are traveling to a higher plane of consciousness. You should do this whether you are practicing by yourself or doing a reading for someone else. You will learn to practice advanced psychic techniques that will allow you to accomplish any goal you may have in mind. Whether it is reading one's emotions, viewing another place on Earth or this universe, receiving messages from another world or time, or locating a lost object, you must always begin with a centering meditation.

Psychometry

Psychometry was first discovered in 1842 and has been used for several centuries. It is the ability to read an object by touch. The object has a history that an individual who is centered and open to energy can read. The psychic will center themselves and open a doorway to allow energy to flow into them. The psychic will either place the object in front of them or hold it in their hands. They are feeling for certain emotions or images to reveal themselves. They can sometimes sense what the person was like, what types of things they did, and possibly how they died. It is up to the psychic to tell the individual what they want them to know, being careful to state only what they know to be the truth. No matter how skilled the psychic is, they may not be able to read all objects all the time.

These abilities - holding an object or being in the same room as someone - may seem simple. However, the amount of mental energy and concentration required is never simple. Remembering to keep still and empty is something you must always do. If your mind begins to wander, you might have to close the door and start over. Hold the meditation as long as you need to feel ready to receive energy.

Automatic Writing

Center yourself as long as you need to. Have a pen and paper ready or use a computer, whatever you are comfortable with. Write whatever thoughts appear in your mind. Soon your conscious thoughts will fade into the background and subconscious thoughts will flow out of your fingertips. Keep writing for as long as you choose or for as long as your thoughts continue. Many psychics who use this method don't know what they have written until they read it later.

Doodling is another form of automatic writing since it is generally not consciously focused. One of the most common doodles is the spiral, which is associated with sacred geometry. It's suggested that if you suffer from emotional problems, you shouldn't attempt to automatic write. Because your frequency is lower due to emotional problems, you are likely to attract a lower-frequency entity. Similarly, if you seem to have constant drama in your life, you shouldn't try to channel. To help you write, it's important to divert your focus, shifting the brain from left brain logical to right brain intuitive. Act as if you are getting ready to write; place pen to paper, then turn your attention to something else. Most people will write something coherent. Messages may be written in a different language or in a writing style unrecognized by the writer, and signed by somebody else.

If you feel comfortable, you will probably find out who is writing through you. If you start to feel the least bit uncomfortable with either the information you are receiving or the entity writing through you, stop. If it feels as though more than one entity is trying to write through you, ask them nicely to be patient and let you get to them one at a time. Be sure to get a name.

Channeling

Channeling is simply receiving images, sounds, or feelings from another plane. Clairaudience is the ability to hear messages from a higher being or plane. The psychic can hear different kinds of voices: whispers or a clear, loud voice, yet no one else is in the room. Clairsentience or psychic empath is the ability to read others' emotions. Those with this ability can pick up on others' feelings, intense emotions, anger, hatred, or signs of stress. They can expertly read body language. Wherever the empath goes to work, the grocery store, or a party, or simply remains at home, they can read the environment. They can read the feelings throughout the room and know what others are feeling.

Finally, clairvoyance, known as clear seeing, is the ability to see images from other planes. Such people can see the future, past, and present. The third eye is responsible for this ability. Focusing on this chakra will help enhance the images. The images might be sharp and in focus or blurry and cloudy.

Dowsing

Dowsing is searching for knowledge or something hidden from view with the aid of hand-held tools. Dowsing began as a means of finding underground water, which isn't surprising because water is a necessity man needs. What many people don't realize is that it can also be used to find metals or ores, gemstones, oil, gravesites, and sometimes missing persons. Anyone is capable of dowsing with the right training and tools. As with many psychic abilities, children tend to demonstrate a natural flair for dowsing. The tools used are basically an extension of a person's natural ability, allowing them to detect things they couldn't otherwise. Here are some tools used for dowsing:

V Rod: These were once made from forked twigs; now a V rod can be made from any springy material, such as wood, cane, plastic, or metal. The V rod will twitch upward when it detects something.

Angel Rods: Angel rods consist of two L-shaped rods; the dowser holds the rod by the short arm with the long section parallel to the ground. When the dowser finds something underground, the longer sections will cross.

Wand: This is a long rod that is held in the hand and that moves in circular or oscillating movements when it detects something.

Pendulum: A pendulum is usually a crystal attached with twine to a rod where it can swing freely. It can react in various movements and is usually used with charts or maps for distant dowsing.

Extra Sensory Perception

ESP is another form of intuition. The psychic can see the energy bouncing off the cosmos at all times. This ability feels natural, just like breathing. There are different degrees of intuition. An intuitive is a person who can offer advice based on the ability to read the energy in the environment. A medical intuitive is a psychic who can read bodies, whether theirs or someone else's, to determine pain, sickness, or damage. They tune into health problems and heal by using therapeutic massage, reiki, acupressure, or acupuncture. A psychic detective is one who can read energy at crime scenes. ESP is an umbrella term for psychic powers that include telepathy, clairvoyance, precognition, and clairaudience.

ESP was first investigated by J.B. Rhine and his wife, Louisa E. Rhine, at Duke University in the 1930s. Louise worked mainly at collecting accounts of ESP, while J.B. worked in the lab, defining the term ESP and finding ways to test it. He developed Zener cards, which contain the following symbols: circle, square, wavy lines, cross, and star. Five cards containing each symbol were in a deck of 25 cards. J.B. would test a person's ability for clairvoyance by hiding the cards while the psychic tried to guess the order.

Medium

A medium is a psychic who can open their mind and body and communicate with spirits. When a human body dies, the energy within must go somewhere. Many believe that's where spirits come from. These psychics can speak with beings that have passed over and that have a message for loved ones. Most who practice in this field are born with this ability and sense the power from a young age. Voices and feelings come to them effortlessly. Mediums typically channel only people who have recently passed as opposed to people who have been gone for several decades. The Ouija board is a famous form of mediumship that anybody can access. Mediums will sometimes use knocking, rapping, or bell ringing to talk to the deceased. Mediums will also perform séances by going into a trance, and will sometimes channel spirits.

Readers

Psychic readers are people who use tools for readings. They can use any combination of leaves, runes, tarot cards, astrology charts, or numerology charts. Cartomancy, tarot or divination cards, are used by readers to tell others of possible blockages that could keep them from reaching their full potential. Readers often perform palm readings. They use the lines, wrinkles, shapes, and curves of the palm to tell someone's future. This type of reading requires psychic ability.

Scrying

The psychic uses water or shiny surfaces in which to see images. They can also use mirrors or two-way mirrors. The images provide information that the psychic can use to help the individual employing their services. Scrying is not a clearly defined psychic ability. The way it is performed is based on the psychic's own preference. Nostradamus, a French apothecary and psychic, practiced scrying by staring into a bowl of water to see the future.

Telepathy

This is much like a psychic empath. It is not about reading one's emotions. The psychic can read minds and get information from others without speaking. Many psychics who possess this skill can read every person they meet. Very rarely are they not able to break into the minds of people.

Here is a fun way to test whether you are telepathic. Ask a friend (one you can trust not to make fun of you) to sit in a different room with playing cards. Have them turn each card over, one at a time, and strike a bell as they do so. Your friend must mentally tell you what the card is. Whenever you hear the bell, write down what you think the card is. After you have gone through the deck, compare your list with the actual order of the cards. If you get fewer than 20 right, your telepathic gift is limited. If you score between 20 and 30, you have average telepathic ability. If you score over 30, you are completely telepathic.

Trance Channel

This is the epitome of using yourself as an instrument for psychic power. This ability requires the psychic to leave their body and allow someone else to enter it. The psychic will be in an altered state and will typically speak in a different voice. They will be speaking as the person who entered their body. This type of psychic ability is very advanced. It takes intense concentration and practice. Psychics either channel spirit guides or entities. Most are entities because they do not have a physical body. Channels can channel highly evolved beings, meaning they can access people who have been gone for centuries.

There are many ways to use your abilities, all of which require starting with meditation to center your mind.

Meditation is extremely important. Without mastering meditation, it will be virtually impossible to practice advanced abilities.

"Once you decide to devote the time and energy necessary for learning how to unlock it, you will discover that within you is an untapped psychic power that is more powerful than the greatest wind or highest sea." – Tana Hoy

3

Ups and Downs of Being an Empath

Being an empath is definitely not easy. It is human nature to fear insight and new information. Anything new threatens one's current identity and means opening up more and more. The greatest threat to the ego is its demise in which humans no longer need a separate identity, and are instead absorbed into the sea of oneness.

Empaths get a small taste of this every day, as they are conscious of the many impulses in the world beyond their own. Imagine all of the things people are thinking, feeling, and experiencing. Most of it is kept under the surface in normal living.

Now imagine what it would be like if all of that information spilled out into the environment. It would be like being pummeled by ocean waves or trying to escape a minefield. The stimuli can be painful, confusing, or simply distracting and unnecessary, and doing very simple daily activities can be a struggle.

Many cultures teach that the world is a place of suffering and pain, and the empath's experience of anguish in the universe certainly supports this. Furthermore, empaths can't always distinguish the source of their feelings and can be easily affected by outside situations.

Some empaths become reclusive because they are so overwhelmed. Something as simple as grocery shopping can become an arduous task requiring great fortitude. Even the empaths who are able to manage on a day to day basis will undoubtedly have issues in other areas.

Relationships are a huge part of most people's lives, and impact just about every aspect. Empaths are so attuned to other peoples' emotions and experiences that it can be hard to know how to handle situations appropriately.

Sometimes, they simply have too much information that muddles and overcomplicates things. Having access to others' secrets can leave people feeling naked or uneasy. Being the only one in the room who sees the true underlying dynamics of a situation can be isolative and lonely.

Unhealthy relationships are especially tough, because it is hard to know where one person ends and the other begins. At these times, it is a challenge to act in the best interests of oneself and the relationship, because the empath is acutely aware of both sets of needs. Unfortunately, the awareness of the other person's needs often overwhelms and outweighs those of the sensitive.

Empaths have a nasty habit of trying to solve conflict at the expense of themselves, and will often make changes to appease the other party. They may have been responding to subtle needs automatically for years, and were not aware of it. Sensitives often go out of their way to balance a situation when doing so is usually not their responsibility.

Feeling another person's stress can be so painful that is easier to try to make them feel better than stand their ground and go against the other person's wishes. Besides, there is often an element of confusion in regards to what is right for the empath, and empaths often suffer from disproportionate guilt and a fear or being "selfish".

Codependency is something many sensitives need to work on. If unaddressed, boundaries become increasingly fuzzier and the relationship becomes increasingly diseased. The empath is not helping, only enabling the dysfunction and denying themselves of health.

Healthier relationships can be a challenge as well. People who are loving and well-intentioned simply may not understand, or misinterpret an empath's experiences. Empaths may be chalked up to being too emotional and told to shake it off. Sensitivities may be dismissed (not necessarily unkindly) and alternate explanations provided.

Loved ones may expect things from empaths that is hard for them to give, and be impatient of the sensitive soul when crowds are avoided, or being in a bad neighborhood is almost intolerable. Some may be sympathetic to empaths, but feel helpless as they watch their friend or family member struggle.

Empaths usually become frustrated at how hard it is to explain what they feel, and how hard it is to make other people get it.

Empaths may hide or minimize their experiences in fear of being judged and rejected, or fear being a burden to others. Others will simply give up trying to make other people understand, and will stick to a few people whom they feel comfortable around.

Something very important that you need to be aware of is how your sensitivity may affect your health. Because empaths absorb energy and are often healers, they tend to sop up large amounts of negative energy. They generally take in the negativity faster than it can be discharged, and the result is disharmony and disease. Depression, anxiety, and mood swings are typical empath problems that stem from retaining too many issues in their environment.

Emotional issues can also be rooted in the complex and painful way they go through life. Other symptoms are more physical in nature, and manifest as conditions like chronic pain, chronic fatigue, and fibromyalgia. Unfortunately, it is not unheard of for empaths to turn to self-destructive behaviors like alcoholism, drug abuse, or overeating as a way to numb themselves from the constant stimulation.

Some sensitives become overly intellectual and cut off from their emotions. They learn how to block everything as a way to survive, including their empathic abilities. Work, home, school, hobbies, etc. are all affected, and functioning in one or more of these areas is typical. A seemingly unrelated issue like financial stress could be a direct correlation to the empath's difficulty focusing and performing on the job.

While reading through this you might think that living as an empath is a huge challenge, and it sure can be. However, it isn't all bad! The empath's life is, if nothing else, highly interesting. And it is misleading to portray all of these gifted individuals as miserable souls who never quite get the hang of coping with life, or as people who won't trust themselves or develop their potential. This is true of some, but there are always those who cultivate their talents and live a fulfilling life.

Sensitive people often have parents or other family members with similar proclivities, and these adults may recognize the behavior for what it is early on. Fortunate empaths will have adults who help them understand and cope with their sensitivity. Even ones who do not have this head start may later in life find peers who are either empaths as well or encouraging to them.

Still others will simply figure it out as they go and adapt well, whether or not they have the words to describe what is happening. And there are always the tenacious who refuse to listen to what other people say and eventually blossom through determination. An empath may manifest as a socially awkward person who avoids crowds, but it could also be a vivacious creature with a lust for life, or a quiet, content, introspective soul.

The word "struggle" has a negative connotation, but it is foolish to assume that struggling is fundamentally unhealthy. In life, stress can be either negative or positive. Negative stress is not constructive, and damages the wellbeing of an individual. Living in a polluted city where cancer rates are far above the national average is stressing the system, and causing disease that could easily be prevented.

Positive stress can be likened to the massive amounts of pressure carbon endures to become a diamond. When people are sore and grumbling after exercising muscles they did not know they had, their pain is a sign of extra strain placed on the system. But this stress is clearly advantageous, and part of a larger plan to increase vigor and strength.

Many serious spiritual practitioners undergo severe ordeals of physical and emotional discomfort to test their stamina. Fasting, sleep deprivation, and exposure to the elements are not unheard-of ways to transcend one's perceived limits, and discover a wealth of previously unimaginable power within. Likewise, the stress associated with being an empath is not necessarily negative.

Life is full of lessons, and the most valuable ones are often painful. The trials may unlock something deep inside that otherwise would have lain dormant. What appears to be negative stress can be transformed into positive stress, but discretion must be used to prevent unnecessary suffering.

Living life as an empath could be described as both a blessing and a curse. Feeling life on a deeper level gives a greater appreciation of existence, but the confusion and awareness of the world's pain is definitely thorny. Yet, this description is shallow at best, and does not speak to the treasures awaiting the empath who learns to gain control over their facilities. Life is a strange, surprising thing and, just when it seems that nothing new can be found, there is yet another discovery.

Being an empath means that you are instinctually attuned to the deeper layers of life, and that you have greater access to experiencing them. Committing to the exploration of such baffling territory can be frightening and overwhelming at first, and you may find yourself longing to be "normal". Being gifted involves making certain sacrifices, and sacrificing the comfort of belonging to the mainstream will be worth it for the much more satisfying rewards ahead.

Empaths are often natural healers, and can be adept physicians, nurses, midwives, chiropractors, massage therapists, and energy healers. For those with sensitivities to plants and animals, gardening or animal training may be second nature. The arts may be the perfect avenue to express the empath's experience of the universe. Their access to wisdom gives them insight that can be of use to others, and being a sensitive soul can make one a superb partner, child, parent, coworker, supervisor or friend.

Being an empath means developing an unusual degree of closeness in healthy relationships. The intimacy, be it physical, emotional, or spiritual, is much more intense, and there is a degree of fulfillment that comes from such a close union that can be difficult to describe. These relationships are not always with other people. They can also be with nature, animals, plants, stones, or the universe at large.

Others will answer the call to spiritual studies and find their niche. Not all will feel the need to be open about their abilities, and instead lead quiet, fulfilling lives full of richness. People who live and speak the truth of the universe are far more beneficial to society than all of the wealthy philanthropists put together.

Empaths are especially attuned to the beauty of creation, and their recognition automatically affects the world by raising the collective vibration of humanity to a higher level. So, as an empath you are full of potential — now the task at hand is learning to accept your gift, and transform it into a positive, purposeful way of being.

4

Awakening Your Psychic Abilities

Throughout elementary school, people learn that they each have at least five common senses – sight, smell, touch, sound, and taste. All of these senses are crucial in everyday life. That is because they all work together to inform our brain about what is going on around us. However, it is a fact that human beings have far more than five senses.

Apart from helping us to communicate and interact with each other, the five senses also serve to keep us safe by warning us of any impending danger. Although these five senses are the traditionally recognized senses, there are other subtle external senses that most people do not even think about. Examples of such senses are:

1. Proprioception

In simpler terms, proprioception is the sense of movement and space. This sense helps people's brains to know where a person's body because the sense triggers movement and position of limbs and muscles. Proprioception helps a person to touch and feel themselves even with their eyes closed. In addition, it enables a person to walk down a street or up the steps without the person having to look at each step. Clumsy and butterfingered people may have poor proprioception.

2. Equilibrioception

Equilibrioception sense and of course, gravity are the reasons you do not fall when you increase your walking pace or running. Equilibrioception is the sense of balance that enables people to maintain body balance when they move or increase their pace.

3. Thermoception

Thermoception describes the sense that helps to know whether something is hot or cold. It enables people to know the difference between heat and cold. On the one hand, the cold receptors are essential in the sense of smell and in telling the direction of the wind. On the other hand, the heat receptors are conscious infrared emission or radiation

4. Nociception

Nociception refers to the sensation of pain. That explains why a person may avoid touching a sharp needle or sit too close by the fire. Without these pain receptors, human beings could do many precarious things without being aware of the dangers.

Therefore, nociception helps to draw people's attention to hazards and drive them to avoid such risks.

5. Magnetoreception

Magnetoreception, in other words, refers to directional awareness. That is the sense that enables people to tell the direction they are facing, based on the earth's magnetic field.

Therefore, one may ask, where do psychic abilities come in?

Psychics have the mental ability to read the minds of other people or to see the future. Psychics also have the capacity to discern information that the traditional senses cannot figure out through extrasensory perception, or the 'sixth sense'.

Are you a psychic? You can know by reading the list below, of psychic abilities that exist in the real world.

Aura reading: Aura means the air or the atmosphere around a person. When you move very close to someone, you can almost feel the heat radiation from the energy that is within his or her body. Therefore, an aura reader has the ability to read other people's energies.

Channeling: Describes the ability to translate messages from the spirits into human words. Channeling is a form of communication between human beings and spirit beings.

Clairaudience: A clairaudient is a psychic who hears and takes in messages directly from spirits.

Claircognizance: Refers to the intuitive ability to know something without reading or hearing people talk about it.

Clairgustance: Points to the ability to smell or taste without putting anything in one's mouth

Clairolfactance: Defines the ability to perceive scents from the spiritual world. A psychic who relies on this ability has a unique capability to smell things that other people cannot recognize.

Clairsentience: Also, called psychic sensing is the ability to receive information through sensing or feeling subtle energies.

Clairvoyance: Denotes the ability to perceive things that are secret to the traditional human senses.

Divination: Infers to the ability to obtain knowledge about the future or unknown events through supernatural means.

Dowsing: Implies the ability to locate water, minerals, and other underground materials using a dowsing or divination rod.

Electrokinesis: Describes the ability to control energies, electric currents, and to generate electricity with the mind. If you make lights flicker when you walk into a room, chances are you are electrokinetic.

Precognition: Refers to the ability to see future events either through vision or intuition or both.

Psychokinesis - Also called telekinesis, is the ability to influence physical objects through mind power, without making any physical contact with the object. Have you ever moved or bent a spoon just by staring at it?

Psychometry - Also, called psychoscopy is the ability to know about a person or an object just by physical touch.

Pyrokinesis - The psychic ability to create and control fire with the mind

Postcognition - Also known as retrocognition is the psychic ability to know about events that took place in the past

Telesthesia - Also known as remote sensing, is the ability to tell whether an event has happened, or is happening just by intuition

Telepathy – This is the ability to transfer information to another person without any physical interaction

Thoughtography – This is the psychic ability to draw or to inscribe photographic-film-like images from one's mind onto material surfaces

Tips to Awaken Your Psychic Abilities

A human being is made up of the body, the mind/soul, and the spirit. However, most people do not know how they can connect to their spirit self – their inner selves. Connecting with the inner self has to do with gradually attuning one's psychic or intuitive abilities.

Important to note is the fact that psychic awakening does not happen in an instant. One has to wait for the divine moment in which this sense will activate. However, one can slowly exercise their psychic abilities as they await the awakening.

Here are ways one can stimulate their psychic abilities:

1.   Have peace in your mind

In general, the connection starts by having peace in your mind. Peace makes it possible for one to begin to link with their psychic. Frustration, stress, and fear can hold one from connecting with their inner being. That is because when one is desperate and worried about their connection, then the link will not happen.

However, it is important to note that some people are fortunate to establish that connection even though they are not in a state of peace and calm.

2.   Decalcify the pineal gland

This is a pineapple-like part of the brain that has the role of releasing melatonin, the hormone that directs a person's cycle of sleep and waking up. The pineal gland also works together with the hypothalamus gland to control the body's hunger, thirst, sexual desires, and the aging process. Too much calcium in the pineal gland, therefore, decreases melatonin synthesis, and this brings about neurological disorders, depression, and anxiety.

Consequently, one should use essential seed oils, chlorophyll-rich foods, lemon water, apple cider vinegar, and refrain from the following: using tap water because the water contains fluoride; using kinds of toothpaste that have fluoride; eating processed foods; and wearing sunglasses most of the time when in the sun and try sun gazing.

Additionally, the person should sleep in complete darkness at night when sleeping; place crystals that have violet and indigo hues between their eyebrows during meditation for about 20 minutes; and finally, exercise third eye meditation by drawing their eyes toward the third eye and focus at the center. Lastly, one should remember to eat pineapple!

3. Meditation

In meditation, one should learn how to breathe deeply through their nose, hold their breath, and finally breathe out slowly. One should do this process repeatedly, taking three seconds for each step.

Once one starts feeling at peace and relaxed, they can go into their regular breathing pattern. During meditation, one should think about happy memories and thoughts. Even better, one can fall asleep while meditating and allow their mind to sink in meditation in that way.

4. Spending time with nature

Spending time with nature strengthens your mind's capacity to relieve stress and toxic thoughts. The quiet moments one spends with nature connect the person's mind to the calmness around.

As a result, one is able to experience peace within themselves and can feel connected to their psychic selves. When one walks on the grass with bare feet, they become one with the ground beneath their feet. Touching the leaves of trees and smelling the flowers helps one to absorb the scents of nature, which bring tranquility in one's mind. Therefore, one could go out, feel the breeze, and get familiar with the sounds of nature!

5. Spending time in public places

One could go to a restaurant, visit a mall, or sit at the airport and observe people as they are walking past and going about their duties. The person could then try to imagine what the people are saying to each other by following the movement of their lips and noticing non-verbal cues. In so doing, one can tell whether there is love or tension between people.

Following in this manner, a person is exercising their third eye and thereby working his or her higher intuition by making a story about two people, or about a group of people, based on how the person is feeling about them.

6. Pay attention to your dreams

When one is asleep, the conscious mind is relaxed and inactive. However, the subconscious mind remains active and broadcasts images and events to the brain in the form of dreams.

The subconscious mind navigates between spaces and spiritual realms. Therefore, one should keep a journal of their dreams as he or she becomes more acquainted with their dream world and their subconscious mind.

7. Visualize your chakras

The word 'chakra' is a Hindu word for a wheel of spinning energy. A chakra is the energy powerhouse that provides one with different ways to obtain psychic information.

A human being has seven chakras running from the base of the spine to the top of the head, which is controlled by spiritual principles that one can use to develop harmony, happiness, and well-being. These chakras are in the form of seven different colors, with each color representing different functions.

When a person suffers from emotional stress or physical problems, the chakras become blocked because the energy system cannot flow freely.

8. Trust your instincts

The more one exercises their intuition, the clearer their insights will become. Most people usually gave gut feelings on certain occasions without realizing that the gut feeling is their psychic ability guiding them.

The more one pays attention to their gut feeling and follows its leading, the more he or she is able to rely on their intuition more than on anything else.

9. Enroll in psychic awakening classes

It is imperative for one to sign up for classes where spiritual improvement courses at taken. The classes could be online, or those taught in person. These classes will enable one to develop consistency as they uncover their unique psychic abilities.

Therefore, one should look for classes that have sound spiritual teachers who will resonate with the person.

5

Psychic Protection

When you have psychic abilities, you have to learn how to protect yourself, your life, and your loved ones from spirits. I have discussed how there are spirits out there who want to do nothing but bring chaos and turmoil to your life. You have to look at it like this if there are good spirits, then there have to be bad spirits. There could not be one without the other. So, when you are trying to contact the good spirits, you open yourself up to the bad ones too.

You see, all spirits are attracted to you because they know they can communicate with you. You give off a sort of light in the spirit world. It is when bad spirits take notice of this light that you have to be careful. You see, each of these spirits has a different purpose, they all come to cause problems in your life, but they cause different types of issues.

When you first realize that a bad spirit has gotten close to you, it may be something like a creepy feeling. Your hair may stand up on the back of your neck or your arms. You just get the feeling of uneasiness. If this is left unchecked, the spirit will only grow stronger. Usually, it will start to show itself in dark places, and you may see a darker than the dark spot in the corner of your house. You may see something run by out of the corner of your eye, or you may just get the feeling that you are being watched. If you allow it to get this far, you must act at this point, or it will only get worse. I will discuss with you what to do later in the part.

If you continue to allow the spirit in your life, you may be awoken at night to strange noises or the feeling that someone is standing over your bed. There are times that you will be able to see a figure depending on how strong the spirit is at this point. Blankets may get pulled off of you while you are sleeping, or you may feel like someone has touched you.

Useful Abilities of Different Empaths

Psychic Abilities

Some empaths have psychic abilities. Environmental, physical/medical, animal, plant, and intuitive empaths all possess psychic abilities to some degree. This special type of ability goes beyond just sensing what those around an empath is going through. Empaths with psychic abilities can often sense what is going to happen to someone despite being miles away from them. They will often be hit suddenly with a flood of sensations that alerts them about what someone else is going through even though they are nowhere near this person. An empath's heightened senses and high levels of empathy can result in them developing psychic abilities or a sixth sense. Empaths who go on to develop their empath gift may find that their psychic abilities come out more clearly.

Visions

The heightened sense of an empath allows them to look at things from a different perspective. They are able to focus on the finer details of a situation or person in order to understand what is going on around them truly and in the other person's life. This ability allows them to tune out the other noise in order to find a deeper meaning and finding the key factors that need one's attention. Not all empaths are able to develop this ability to its fullest when developed, and if an empath does develop this ability but lacks the understanding of how to utilize it properly, they put themselves at a greater risk of being taken advantage of.

Intuition

Everybody has some level of their own intuition, but much like everything else, an empath has a stronger awareness or intuition. When an empath has a strong sense of self, they are able to develop their intuitive abilities fully. While intuitive empaths naturally have this ability, other empaths can tap into their intuition as well. This intuition can help guide an empath and allows them to address certain situations better. With this ability, empaths are able to diffuse negative situations before they occur, and this ability also allows them to have better judgments about people.

An empath's intuition is almost never wrong. Only when an empath lacks the self-respect and trust in themselves will their intuition be off. For this reason, it is important for an empath to gain a better understanding of all their abilities and unique characteristics to utilize their intuitive abilities better.

Telepathy

This is an ability that some empaths are able to strengthen. Telepathic abilities allow empaths to understand the thoughts of another person fully. This helps them know exactly where emotional responses are coming from. Many empaths use this ability to help an individual heal further and recognize their own thought patterns that cause them to have negative or positive emotional responses.

Natural Healing

An empath's ability to connect with others makes them natural healers as well. Because so many individuals seem just to be drawn to empaths and feel more comfortable around them, empaths are able to really listen and understand what an individual needs in order to heal. While physical empaths will be able to heal individuals on a different level, by being able to share what changes they need to make to recover from an illness or health condition, all empaths are able to do this to some varying degree.

Seeing through Lies

Empaths can easily pick up on when someone is dishonest. Whether the words you say are a lie or the way you present yourself to others is covering who you truly are, an empath knows you're lying. Some empaths can even identify what you are lying about. Empaths tend to avoid people they know to be dishonest as these people tend to give off negative energies and, therefore, can leave an empath feeling ill or extremely fatigued.

Heightened Senses

Empaths are easily overstimulated due to their heightened senses. This is why an empath prefers to choose environments that are calmer and quieter. Bright colors, lights, and noise can increase the anxiety that an empath already feels. This heightened sensitivity to external objects can often add to the overwhelming feeling that empaths struggle to cope with when they are in larger crowds. It is also why they tend to be very careful about where they work, as many work environments can trigger these senses, making it impossible for them to be productive.

Creativity

Many empaths have highly creative talents. They tend to be able to look at things from a unique perspective more easily and can be incredibly innovative. For this reason, empaths can also make incredible successful entrepreneurs. Music, art, and other creative outlets that let an empath be hands-on are things they tend to thrive at.

Most empaths find themselves in some sort of creative industry. This is because of their ability to look at things differently, think of innovative ideas, and have a deeper sense of being able to understand what is possible—meaning they can take simple ideas other than their own or in collaboration with others and turn those ideas into something tangible. Empaths are dreamers, but they do not just simply dream; they quietly set out to make their dreams a reality.

The Downside of Being an Empath

Empaths can be easily manipulated, especially by those who are aware of their abilities. When a toxic personality, like a narcissist, identifies an empath, they will try to take advantage of them and take control of them. Empaths naturally attract others, and negative people are often more attracted to an empath than the positive ones. Due to the caring and giving nature of an empath, this keeps them on constant guard. While they trust their intuition, and many can often spot these negative or toxic people, this doesn't put a hold on their deep desire to want to help them.

Many empaths tend to feel incredibly insecure about themselves. This insecurity is brought on not just because of the energy they absorb but because their abilities are often misunderstood. They often feel like outsiders and will try to hide what they are capable of in order to fit in. Empaths are also people pleasers. This deep desire to help everyone they come in contact with can lead to them having a victim mentality or being codependent.

Empaths need their alone time but also tend to retreat or hide in it. They have a hard time battling with this facade they put on in front of everyone else while known deep in their nature they were born to help others. This is a conflicting stage for an empath. It is a stage where many ignore their abilities and settle for a life they are never really comfortable with. On the other hand, some learn to embrace their abilities and take the first step to embrace who they are and what they feel is their purpose.

Now you have a clear understanding of which empath you are. Do you have an increased awareness just people or can you feel the energy of other things like animals and plants? Knowing which type of empath you are will help develop those specific abilities that come with that type of empath. You also now know what additional abilities you possibly possess as an empath but haven't accessed yet. In the next chapter, we will cover the specific way you can develop your empathy so you can begin to live up to your full potential.

6

"The Energy Vampires"

Have you ever come across someone who always leaves you feeling listless and drained? Chances are you have encountered an energy vampire. They could be anyone. Friends, coworkers, even family.

Energy vampires usually lack empathy. They feed off of your psychic energy, and your willingness to care for and listen to them. This parasitic relationship may or may not be intentional. These toxic people can suck the positivity right out of a room by merely walking in.

The super toxic ones like narcissists go as far as using your need for validation to convince you that you are flawed in some way. They say stuff like "Man up," or "You are way too sensitive" to make you doubt yourself. My advice? Treat them like gum under your Louboutins. If you find that too difficult, there are always air pods.

The Dine and Dash Cycle

The phrase "dine and dash" means what you think it means. It's the equivalent of eating at a restaurant and then taking off without paying for the meal. The dine and dash cycle is a strategy used by toxic people who are in dire need of emotional healing, and want a shortcut to said healing without being held accountable for it.

Your generosity is a daily banquet from which they eat to their fill, draining you, and giving nothing back. You are stuck in limbo, yet you cannot complain. Their evil innovative minds come up with the most creative methods to scare you into submission to a point where you begin to ask yourself if you are not the one imagining the pain you feel.

You are perpetually attracted to damaged people, or maybe it is the other way around. Don't be surprised that as an empath, your constant self-doubt and low self-esteem will sometimes place you in a painful cycle of wound-mate relationships with toxic people, on account of the emotional issues you both share and haven't healed yet.

Kinds of Energy Vampires

The Narcissist

Like the perfume Chanel number 5, they are a classic. These ones suffer from a fixation with their own selves. They are drawn to you because you fuel their need for power. They enjoy the game of catch and release. Just like you, they are intuitive, but they're the Joker to your Batman. Unless your throat doesn't get parched from feeding them constant praise, then skedaddle away from these kinds of people.

The ultimate narcissist block: The best way to deflate their ever-rising egos is to put some distance between you two. It does not mean that you care less. It means you have decided to put yourself first. They may become ice cold and unforgiving at first, and you will feel really, really bad, but I suggest some Oolong tea. Something tells me before the cup gets too cold, they will come back to sweet talk you into their self-absorbed world. Don't fall for it, though. Wait them out, and they will use the ace up their sleeve: Gaslighting. This is when they say and do things that alter your perception of yourself and reality just enough for you to question if you should be in a psych ward. Don't believe the hype. You are definitely not crazy.

The Martyr

Coming a close second in the mix would be the ones that are always playing the victim card. If you have met anyone in this category, you will agree without question that they are just downright annoying. Like a pebble stuck in your shoe.

You can only play the victim for so long until everyone realizes you are the problem. If you are the kind of empath who is always seeking to "fix" people, then that means you carry on problems heavier than what you can bench press at your local gym.

The martyr's "woe is me" mentality makes them always imagine others as the cause of their distress. The worst part? They are extremely difficult to please! The most popular phrases in a victim's dictionary are "yes, but" and "no, but." "It wasn't my fault" and "you are the only one who can help me with insert-crippling-worry-here" are also tracks they love to put on repeat.

Some of these victims enjoy their helplessness. It's a drug to them. Most times, they go out of their way to make friends with people who will abuse, manipulate them so they can get a healthy dose of pain.

The ultimate martyr block: Like the narcissist, you need to protect your energy from the martyrs by setting clear boundaries. Don't snap at them, as much as you may want to. Not unless you need a bucket of tears to flush the toilet with or something. Save the planet, stop wasting Kleenex, and learn to say no with a smile on your face. Understand that you can't fix everyone. You are not their therapist. They are not your pet project.

Don't encourage them or their complaints. Change the topic. I find the weather is always a good choice. Adopt a closed-off body language. You can do this by standing your ground and crossing your arms across your chest while keeping eye contact at a minimum. That way, if you tell them you are busy or held up with something, they will get the message loud and clear.

As for phone calls, keep those short and to the point. Long phone calls are a sure-fire way to get them comfortable enough to start talking about issues that are best discussed with their therapist.

The Domineering Lord

These ones are the weakest. Ironic right? They get off on intimidating others. If there is one thing I learned from my mother, it's that you don't have to weaken others to be strong.

These types of vampires are in the active business of seeking for willing subjects they can bend and break to their sovereign will. Some research articles suggest that they were either bully as children, or bullied as children.

The domineering vampires are the biggest critics you will ever see. They have a lot of unsolicited opinions which they do not hesitate to offer, regardless of your need for peace and quiet. They say stuff like "You should have," or "You could have," and then they proceed to hound you consistently about what you have done wrong in their eyes.

As an empath, you tend to take their opinions and criticisms to heart. This chips away at your self-confidence until you end up defining yourself by their ridiculous standards for perfection.

The ultimate domineering lord block: Don't hesitate to assert your opinion. Don't be afraid to disagree. You might be tempted to play the victim during moments of criticism, but take a deep breath and firmly tell them what you think.

The Chatterbox.

Nonstop talkers are annoying in general. They drain your life force with the endless barrage of words coming from their mouth. A minute in their presence feels like a year because of all that talk!

They also do not understand the concept of personal space. You can't hide from these ones. Like badgers, they have mapped out all your hiding spots.

Excessive talking should be a legitimate addiction because these people love to hear themselves talk. If there were a Chatterers Anonymous, they'd fit right in. You, the fantastic listener that you are, are always a magnet for these chronic talkers. Unfortunately, your gentle nature does not allow you to tell them to buzz off if you have had enough of their spiel, because you don't want to sound rude or insensitive.

The ultimate chatterbox block: Learn the art of "effective interruption." The chatterboxes do not respond to nonverbal cues. If you think shifting your feet from side to side or looking impatient will save you, you have another think coming. Find your funny bone. It's all about using tact and humor to tell them you have had enough and have other places to be. Need to get a word in edgewise? Say something like, "If you don't mind, I have something to add."

The Passive Aggressive

These vampires are the Martha Stewarts of the world, and beneath all their sugary exterior is a Molotov cocktail ready to go off. Here's a scenario for you:

Amanda knew she would be getting home late following a meeting at work that took longer than expected. She texted her boyfriend Ryan to say she would be home late, but there were leftovers in the fridge in case he was hungry and got home before her. Ryan texted back a single word: "Okay." This looks like perfectly normal behavior, right?

Well, Amanda gets home and tries to kiss Ryan, but his lips are sealed tight. Amanda: What's a wrong babe? Is everything okay?

Ryan: Yeah.

Amanda: Okay... Mama bear wants a kiss welcome. Ryan: I need to brush my teeth first.

Amanda: You never minded before.

Ryan: (Smiling) I don't usually mind, but today is a tad different. I burnt my hand, preparing dinner, you see. I hope you were able to pick up my dry-cleaning with your extended workday and all. Oh, and maybe next year, you'll remember my birthday faster than my need for a hearty supper.

See that? Hostility beneath Ryan's very pleasant facade.

It is a common mistake to assume narcissists and passive aggressors are the same kinds of the vampire because most of the time, their traits bleed into each other like some weird oil painting. Comment on their behavior, and they will be quick to dismiss it as a joke. You often find them sulking in a corner when they don't get their way, but when asked, they claim nothing is wrong.

The ultimate passive-aggressive block: There is a pattern. Recognize it. Your abilities as an empath ensure your intuition is never wrong. Trust it, especially when they are hiding their anger. Monsters may not be real, but their anger definitely is, even if you can't see it yet.

Limit your reactions to their opinions. They are usually flawed in some way. You need to see that their criticisms are just a true reflection of how they perceive themselves. Remind them of the log in their own eyes. The spoke in yours is your business to mind.

The Stage Actor

If you were not so attuned to emotions and energy signals, you would find this group of energy vampires entertaining. Every day is a carnival. The world is their stage, and it is hardly big enough. These people need drama like they need oxygen, and if they don't have it, they create it.

The ultimate stage actor block: Remain calm. They find this infuriating. When they cannot evoke a reaction from you, they tend to drift towards someone else who feeds their need to create trouble. A lot of distance is also vital as a protection strategy. Set firm limits to ensure open lines of communication. Allow them to stir their crisis cauldron.

7

Shielding & Clearing your Energy

Shielding means protecting yourself against negative, harsh, and lower energies. It is a way to make sure that your energy remains clean and high, especially when you're working in or travelling through a harsh environment. Below are some of the most effective ways to shield your energy:

Crystals and Gemstones

Crystals are powerful stones, rocks and minerals that can protect, magnify and transmute various energies. Holding, wearing, sleeping or working near these protective gemstones help repel negative energy and enhance positivity. Some of the most effective shielding crystals are the following:

Amethyst

This beautiful purple gemstone is excellent for protection and purification. It enhances intuition, helps release addictions, improves spiritual awareness and lifts the energy in you and around you. At the same time, it wards off negative energy -

both ethereal and spiritual. Having this crystal around will greatly help you in coping with your empathic abilities.

Blue Topaz

This crystal will help you think clearly and ease the tension brought about by your work, social or love life. It will also help you communicate your thoughts, desires and pleas to the universe, and see the bigger picture.

Black Tourmaline

This powerful protection gemstone is particularly helpful for empathic healers. It fends off all negative energy, including those that are being purposefully directed at an individual and general negative energy coming from the world around you.

Green Aventurine

This crystal possesses great vitality, making it an excellent healing stone for any situation related to health, friends, finances, growth, confidence and everything else. This is an important stone to have in an empath's arsenal.

Obsidian

Wearing this gorgeous black gemstone will help you ground yourself. It deflects anger, psychic attacks and negativity.

Citrine

This stone represents happiness and creativity. If you're feeling down or stuck in a creative block, this lovely yellow stone can help you. It gives a powerful boost for all things related to finances, abundance and prosperity. It also manifests radiant energy, which pushes away negativity and attracts positive vibes.

Lepidolite

Lepidolite enhances the power of other nearby stones and crystals, and relieves anxieties that commonly plague empaths. This stone is well-known for its peace, power and ability to foster love, luck and sleep.

Malachite

Malachite is perfect if you want to eliminate emotional blockages and pressures that may occur when dealing with stressful situations. This gemstone has a great tendency to absorb negative emotions you may be keeping inside.

Rose Quartz

The energy of this pale pink crystal is gentle, calm and compassionate. It provides a feeling of genuine, unconditional love, and protects you in romantic relationships. It also heals and soothes the heart chakra, and pushes away all the negative feelings around you.

Clear Quartz

This stone is highly versatile and can act as a powerful amplifier of any frequency, including the natural electromagnetic frequency (EMF) in the human body. This clear crystal can refract sunlight into rainbows, and deflect negative energy and vibrations.

Smoky Quartz

This crystal releases negativity from your past relationships. Place it close to your bed and let it do its job while you sleep. You will wake feeling lighter and with a more positive outlook.

Lapis Lazuli

This stunning blue stone is another excellent protector, but its influence is more inclined to spiritual growth. It helps you maintain an objective attitude and take others' actions lightly and not too personally. This stone helps keep your energy unbound and your mind clear of muddled thoughts, great for use in the office or other workplaces.

Jade

This is a popular crystal amongst lovers, but is great for empaths, too. Jade helps balance the opposing energies of romantic partners, and prevent them from inflicting harm on themselves and others during spats and quarrels.

Turquoise

Turquoise drives negative energy out of your space. It creates a stronger, more resilient bond between your physical body and energy field. Even a small piece of this stone can go a long way, filling an entire home with positive vibrations and soothing energy. Many people consider turquoise as the ultimate anti-negativity gemstone.

Unakite

Although not as popular as the other stones, Unakite can be a great inclusion in your arsenal. This crystal helps balance your emotions and bring your spirit close to the other side so that you can stay connected to late loved ones who may be checking on you every once in a while.

Zoiste

Zoiste is another uncommon yet valuable crystal. It is perfect for artistic empaths because it promotes creativity, individuality and connectedness to other people. Many artistic empaths are introverted and tend to shut everybody out. This stone reminds the spirit that human contact is not only important, but can also be fun.

Fossils

While not exactly a crystal or gemstone, fossils are also important to an empath's wellbeing. Fossils will keep you strong and grounded, and constantly remind you that energy is fluid and everything will change inevitably.

Picking the Perfect Crystals

After deciding on what crystals, you need, you will then have to pick out the right ones. Certain stones work better for some, but not as well for others. Follow these three steps to find the perfect crystals for you.

1. Set your intention.

Before you begin the process of finding the perfect gemstone or crystal, you must first set an intention. Speak inside yourself or aloud about what crystal you're hoping to find. Example: "Amethyst, thank you for becoming my new crystal. Please show yourself to me."

2. Follow your senses.

As empaths, we have strong intuitive senses and physical senses. Intuitive senses include Clair cognizance (clear knowing), clairgustance (clear tasting), clairalience (clear smelling), clairsentience (clear feeling), clairaudience (clear hearing), and clairvoyance (clear seeing). Turn on all of these senses when picking your perfect gemstone.

3. Wait for a feeling

There are times when a gemstone or crystal just stands out among the others. If you come across a stone, which keeps grabbing your attention, then that might be the one for you. Also, some crystals vibrate or emit a certain kind of energy when handled by the right person. Wait for that feeling.

Angelic Shielding

You can appeal to the protector Archangel Michael to protect you with his royal purple and royal blue light. Say this either silently or aloud, "Archangel Michael, please shield me with your protective light now." This archangel is limitless, so can instantly protect anyone who calls on him.

You can also call upon God and ask Him to send additional guardian angels to look after you, your home, your loved ones, your friends, or any other important person, thing or place. Angels are infinite in number, and all you need to do is ask and more will come for you.

Clearing

Clearing your energy is as important as shielding it. Whenever you get confused, feel exhausted, or become prone to accidents, take a break to clear your energy. Most of the time, these are signs that you have absorbed too much negativity.

Like shielding, there are different ways to clear yourself and this also includes calling upon Archangel Michael. You can say: "Archangel Michael, I ask of you to clear away all the energies within and around me that aren't of God's light and love." The archangel instantly comes to the aid of everyone who calls on him, for he loves all of us and can help everyone at once.

Another fine way to clear your energy is to take a warm bath enhanced by Epsom salts (sea salts are fine) and essential oils. You can further improve it by adding pure flower essences to your bathwater and surrounding your tub with white candles. The candles will serve as focal points for your genuine intention of clearing yourself.

Massage and similar bodyworks also have excellent clearing abilities, especially if your massage therapist is skilled in relieving physical tension and energy.

Detoxing and tweaking your diet are another effective way to dispel energetic and physical toxins. You can work with juices, supplements or herbs that flush out contaminants and heavy metals attached to the energy toxins in your system.

Consult a naturopath or a trained staff at your local supplements store to get the best recommendations.

Grounding

Grounding means your consciousness is contained inside your body, instead of floating freely above it. Many empaths leave their physical bodies when the earth plane becomes too much to handle. They "go home" inside their consciousness and you can say they are not really "here." It is okay to do this during meditation or dream time, but during your waking hours, remember the reasons you are in your physical body.

Besides wearing obsidian crystal to help you ground yourself, eat organic, non-GMO vegetables such as turnips, onions, carrots, potatoes and radishes. You can also get a foot rub or visualize yourself as a tree, with roots growing out of your feet. Feel the earth's energy connect with the bottom of your feet.

Another way to ground yourself is to connect physically with nature. Take your shoes off and touch the soil, sand, grass or water. This will help you shift your focus back to your physical reality.

8

Developing your Gift

If you are reading this book then you are ready to get started on the road to feeling empowered and confident in yourself! Remember, even the most experienced or naturally gifted psychics didn't start their journey with complete confidence and power; they had to practice often to gradually increase their abilities. The key is to believe in yourself and stay relaxed. Trust in your ability and intuition, even though if you've been raised to ignore it may feel silly at first. Keep noticing subtle things you sense.

Additionally, keep in mind that you should keep practice sessions relatively short, no more than an hour, as longer sessions are unnecessarily draining and exhausting. You can't be expected to keep your focus that long. Once you've lost your focus, concentration, and grounding, any practice you attempt will be ineffective.

A feeling of fear may arise as you begin to have more accurate warnings. This is natural —you're now aware of a plane of reality that humans are not normally in tune with. Part of developing your abilities and confidence is overcoming this fear or uneasiness. If you truly want to become more powerful, fear will only get in your way. Reluctance will hinder you. It's true that not every prediction will be a positive one. You may foresee relationships ending or loss of money or death, and you must accept that these are all a part of life. You must be ready for negative warnings as well.

Another important thing to remember is: don't let skeptics dissuade you. You'll know if you've had a psychic experience that even though it can't be explained by logic, there's no denying its truth. If there are many hardcore logical skeptics in your life, they may mock you or question you, trying to convince you that you're foolish or even crazy. It's important to remain calm and focused; don't let these kinds of people distract you or hinder your abilities. You'll find people like them everywhere, so try to block them out as best you can.

One great technique is writing down potential psychic messages. Try keeping a journal of what you think may be clairvoyant, audient, sentient or cognizant premonitions. Keep track of these recordings and see if anything ever becomes of them – if they're relevant at all. This is an excellent technique for beginners because you can sort out the random bits and pieces from actual psychic messages, and you can start to piece together what a prediction or warning feels like. It may help you to write down how you felt beside each potential message as well.

This can't be reiterated enough. Practice every day. This may sound daunting, but if you keep it up, pretty soon it will come naturally, and you won't even notice you're doing it. If you miss a day or two or more for whatever reason (illness, feeling emotionally drained, etc.), don't worry! Just pick up where you left off and keep testing different techniques and tools. It's not something to panic about if you haven't practiced in a while, you won't lose "the gift" as we all have it, just as your muscles won't disappear if you don't go to the gym for a while. This is just to tell you the best and most effective ways of developing your gift's power.

Another highly effective tool is meditation. If you're practicing daily, try incorporating ten to twenty-minute meditation sessions into your daily routine before you try to interpret anything. This will clear out any emotional blockages, thoughts, worries, or distractions you may have both relevant to psychic practice or about your daily life. It also connects you to a higher plane where your spirit guide(s) and psychic energy reside.

If possible, surround yourself with like-minded people, such as other psychics or people on the same spiritual path as you. If you find people on the same vibrational level, your energy will rise, and this will help you thrive spiritually. Thus, growing your psychic ability. It's also nice to have positive reinforcement from your peers.

Spending time in nature is also a stress reliever to help open your mind. Some of this may just sound like basic life advice that doesn't have much to do with psychic powers. Still, it's impossible to grow as a psychic if you are stressed and emotionally/energetically blocked. Nature is our roots. Nature was here before us, and it will remain here long after we pass. Walk around and realize that, despite all your worries, the trees will still stand steady.

Ask questions of the universe frequently. Whether you're walking down the sidewalk and are wondering whether you should change careers, or you're relaxing in the bath, wondering if your relationship is working out? No matter where you are and what you're wondering, try to become aware of this and consciously ask the universe for advice.

Psychometry is a really easy technique to try. The word may sound complicated, but all it means is reading the energy of an object. Just pick something up that has some meaning you know, like a family heirloom to start, and focus on the energy coming off of it. Clear your mind and see what comes up. Don't force any images, just let them flow. Once you've practiced like this a few times, try transitioning to an object you don't know the history and meaning of. Go to a thrift store and buy an old silver knick-knack or item of jewelry.

Crystal ball scrying is another classic tool used by psychics. It's such a famous item that it's made its way into many movies and it's a universal symbol of psychics. While it is such a famous symbol, it's an art that's tricky to perfect and most likely won't yield immediate or solid results. To start, it's best to do crystal ball scrying in a dimly lit atmospheric space that will allow the mind to relax and wander. Large crystal balls can be quite pricey, but small ones work just as well and are much cheaper. Make sure it's a clear crystal ball and not made of an opaque stone, and that you have some sort of stand for it (wood, glass or stone is preferable to plastic) so that it doesn't just roll off the table. As you gaze into your crystal ball, your focus should be on the middle. Try to have some sort of solid background behind it so that you don't mistake the distortion of any objects or light for images. You should feel yourself entering an almost trancelike state, and it may take a few minutes for the ball to begin to reveal things to you. Remember, relaxation is the key. Light incense or diffuse essential oils and play calming instrumental music if you think this will aid you in getting to the proper state where the ball's secrets will reveal themselves. Take a moment to quiet your mind before you begin. Clear it of any hopes or expectations of what you think will happen or what you think you will see.

Another thing to consider before you begin is, like with your tarot deck, spending time getting familiar with your crystal ball. Hold it, keep it near you, build up that connection. Now that you are ready, your mind calm, your atmosphere set, you can begin gazing. Make sure whatever position you're sitting in to gaze will be comfortable for an extended period as it may take a while for messages to be revealed, or if it's your first time, not at all. You will have to remain in one position for a while to hold your focus. As you gaze, visualize that your mind is as clear as the crystal ball. You'll know a message is incoming when a mist begins to appear. When this happens, do not shift, either physically or mentally. Try to hold focus and keep the connection. Remain calm and still. You will feel yourself and your mind being drawn into the crystal ball, the ball and you are one. Images will appear, but don't interpret them yet. Just take them in, absorb them all one by one as they appear, until they start to fade away. This is when you can break your focus.

Palmistry (or chirology) is another famous symbol of psychic practice, and another useful tool many psychics use to perform readings. It is much easier to master than crystal ball scrying and cheaper than buying a crystal ball or tarot deck. All you need is a person who's willing to let you hold their hands for a short period, and that costs no money at all. You may have even seen your local psychic shop adorned with a neon sign of a hand with all the lines used by palm readers to tell you about your life. Each line represents something different about a person. There's the life line, the half circle starting from the middle of your hand and curving around your thumb. The head line and the heart line, which run parallel to each other (the head line is the lower one, the heart line higher, closer to your fingers). There are also the fate line which cuts through the heart and the head line, but not all people have a fate line. These are just a few of the most basic lines that you can interpret on someone's hand. The life line represents health, injury, major life events, and wellbeing. The head line represents how someone thinks and communicates, how creative or intellectual someone is, and how someone learns. The heart line represents emotion, romance, relationships, mental health, and heart health. The fate line shows how much of someone's life will be controlled by "destiny" or forces outside of their control. Look at your hand and see if you can pinpoint each line. How you read them is based on how the line appears on the hand. Longer and curvier lines mean more emotional and creative. In comparison, straighter and shorter lines show a good handle on emotions and a logical disposition.

9

Psychic Protection Techniques

In this part you are going to be learning all about personal energy management. How to maintain a clear and strong energy field is important. You will also be learning more advanced ways to use energy to filter harsh or negative energies and block psychic attacks.

Visualization is a big part of psychic protection and shielding. Some people wonder how effective it is to create a shield around them. Is this just your imagination? Put your hand out in front of you in a stop hand gesture, now. Okay, what did you do to move your hand out? You just had to think it to direct your energy and thoughts to move your body. Working in the spiritual world is no different. It is just that we are not using physical atoms. The more you do this, the more confident you will get and the more powerful your psychic protection becomes.

Daily Psychic Protection

Many people use psychic protection daily. This usually involves some form of shielding which can be applied in the morning and or at night before you go to sleep. This type of shielding is for general protection from negative energies we encounter in our daily life. It is something I feel all Empaths and highly sensitive people should use. In this part I will show you how to shield yourself and explain the different types of shields you can use.

Daily Aura Clearing

As I hope by now you have realized, we pick up energies every day that do not support us. A buildup of negative energies over time is just a recipe for problems. Like a magnet it can draw negative attention, situations and people if left unchecked.

You could incorporate some kind of aura clearing into your daily routine. Although showering and bathing helps clear the aura, you may want to use visualizations and other practices to make it even more effective. These can also be done any time of the day, as and when you feel you need them. They work well when done in the morning or at night.

Daily Grounding

As explained in the later part, grounding is an important part of psychic protection but is often overlooked. With good grounding you will be less likely to confuse your energy with others. Grounding also helps anchor your shielding so that it is strong and stable for longer.

There are so many ways you can ground yourself and it will all depend on your lifestyle, location and what works for you. Using visualization, such as the Tree of Life Grounding Meditation given in the last part is one way. You can repeat this when needed throughout the day. For a quick refresh you can just say to yourself "I connect to the center of the Earth" and focus on the Iron crystal at the core of the planet.

This can be backed up throughout the day or replaced by the following physical grounding techniques. For these to make a big difference you do need to incorporate them into your daily routine at set times. Something in the morning and something in the evening is more effective.

- Walking outside in nature

- Eating high protein whole foods, like nuts or root vegetables

- Drinking a glass of fresh fruit or vegetable juice

- Showering or bathing

- Laying on the floor or touching the earth

- Doing any kind of physical exercise

- Taking deep, slow breaths

- Walking through a wood, forest or touching a tree

- Walking on the beach

- Walking barefoot on grass, sand or earth

- Handling a grounding crystal or touching natural rock

- Massaging your ear lobes

- Preparing a meal, baking or cooking

- Doing Tai Chi or Qi Gong

- Doing Yoga

Cosmic Energy Shower

For this visualization you are going to be connecting with the cosmic energy of our Galaxy and the Universe. The visualization is really simple and can be done in a couple of minutes if that is all you have. Why not do this while showering or during a five-minute morning or evening meditation?

1. Close your eyes and take a deep breath.

2. Visualize a glowing light source above you and say to yourself "I call forth a Cosmic Energy Shower of silver-white light to cleanse my aura."

3. Visualize this shimmering silver-white light coming down like rain all around you and through you.

4. See it passing through your head, shoulders, arms, hands, chest, lower body, pelvis, legs and down though your feet into the Earth.

5. Allow it to carry any remaining energies that do not serve you down into the Earth for transmutation.

6. When you feel this has been done, open your eyes and take a few moments before doing anything else.

Waterfall Visualization

This is another visualization method to help cleanse your aura, which you might like to try. This one works with the cleansing energy of the water element.

1. Close your eyes and take a few deep breaths.

2. Visualize yourself standing in a pool of water in a forest or jungle. Before you are a beautiful waterfall that cascades into the pool.

3. In your mind's eye step into the waterfall. See and feel it cascade over you, but still allowing you to breathe as normal.

4. Allow it to cleanse away all negative or unbalanced energies. They wash away into the water and are carried far away by a river for purification and healing.

5. When you feel this has been done, open your eyes and take a few moments before doing anything else.

Aura Sprays

You can quickly cleanse your aura using aura sprays. Any spray created for the purpose of cleansing and purification will do. Generally, they will have essential oils like Sage, Lavender or Citrus in them. Some may incorporate Gem essences from cleansing crystals. All you have to do is spray them above your head and around you. Turn around in the fine mist and allow it to clear you of unwanted energies as it descends down to the floor. This is so easy and quick to do.

Cleansing Your Aura with Selenite

This is easiest to do if you have a Selenite Wand. This can be a cut and polished crystal or a raw one. Selenite is a deeply cleansing stone that can rid the aura of harmful energies quickly. Hold your Selenite wand in your dominant hand. Start above your head and working all around you and your aura, sweeping downwards. It's like brushing your aura clean. Do this for the head, then neck and chest area. Then your arms and down your lower body and legs, down to the ground.

TIP: If you have time, keep close to your physical body to cleanse the inner layers of your aura first. Then afterwards start again from the top with your arm stretched out to work on the outer layers of the aura.

What Exactly Is Shielding?

The term shielding or psychic shielding is used throughout this book to refer to working with energy to create a force field around our aura. These shields can filter, block or transmute energies that we do not wish to have around us. A shield is a clearly defined energetic boundary used in psychic protection. These shields work best when they cover all angles, 360 degrees in all directions like a bubble. Shielding can also be applied to a space such as a room or your home.

The Power of Consistency

When you first start using psychic protection shields, it is like anything new. It may not feel natural, it could feel like a chore and you may not feel sure it is even working. The truth is that shielding improves its effectiveness over time and through consistent use. You are going to be building etheric structures on a spiritual dimension. The spiritual world responds to repetition and focused intent. Your long-term consistency will lead to a bulletproof aura. Shielding yourself just becomes a habit, like brushing your teeth.

Positive Thinking & Empowerment

Everything I am about to teach you including all the crystals are not going to be very effective if you are constantly doubting them. Your thoughts create energies and if your energy is contradicting your intention, it will weaken all you do. It's okay to acknowledge your fears but don't dwell on them too long. You are acting now and tapping into your power.

The source of a psychic attack wants you to be scared and weak. Don't give them what they want. Put your spiritual armor on and send a clear message to anyone that's bothering you or who wishes you harm to back off and leave you alone. They have no power over you, unless you let them. Stand up, shield up, remember who you are and take back your power!

When to Use a Protection Shield

How often and when you use shielding is up to you. I do feel that some people need more protection than others, such as highly sensitive people, Empaths and those on a spiritual path. If you fall into one or more of these categories or work with the public, then you should consider daily shielding.

If you don't feel you need that, you can apply shielding in specific situations. This could be before dealing with a particularly negative person, when you visit a busy place or only if you experience a psychic attack.

Everyday Shielding Vs High Strength Shields

For most people and for general use you do not need a high strength shield. The type of shielding that is used on a day-to-day basis is different and more porous. There is no point in using high strength shielding when there is no need for it. This may manifest in people being wary of you because of your overly defensive energy. In some cases, it has an almost 'invisibility cloak' effect, in that people just don't notice you anymore.

High strength shields are needed for anyone experiencing a psychic attack or following one. They can also be used when going into a negative environment, with lots of low vibration energies or people. They can be employed when we feel particularly vulnerable. High strength shields give extra protection when doing spiritual work that is more advanced or that we are not experienced in.

Programming Self-Regenerating Shields

Here is something that very few people will tell you. Most people have no idea that a psychic protection shield should ideally be programmed. This is one of the reasons shielding does not work well or wears off very quickly for some people.

If you program your shield for your personal needs it will work the way you want it to. You also want to make sure that the shield is self-regenerating. The worst form of psychic shielding uses your energy. This can be draining and there is no need to do it. If you feel weak or scared, creating a shield from your energy will not be very effective. The Universe has so many limitless sources of energy that can power your shield and keep it replenished.

The final part of the programming is to set a specific timeframe for it to work. The shield will deactivate or disintegrate at the end of this time. This way there is no need to worry about leaving any old etheric shields lingering around on the Astral Plane or cluttering up your aura when you no longer need them. For daily shielding you can program your shield to last for 24 hours. For a specific situation or high strength shield you could set it for anywhere from 1 to 24 hours. After that, if needed again or if this is for everyday shielding, you just reactivate it.

10

The Key to Controlling Empathy

The key to controlling empathy is to make sure that you are in full awareness of yourself and your own emotions and energy. Every day, all over the world, people are experiencing all kinds of different realities, dramas, partnerships, professions, and family lives that are in flux with all of the other people going through life right beside them.

It is our passion as people to understand ourselves and find solutions to our problems and our needs. With your gift of being an Empath, you can truly embrace and explore what it means to sense and feel these realities, situations, and human bonds in a deeper more heartfelt way.

Being an Empath is a great responsibility and it isn't hard to live this way if you give yourself the tools to empower your ability instead of feeling debilitated by it. There are so many different ways to help your energy stay grounded and balanced. If you continue to practice using these tools and techniques regularly, you will no longer have to think about or study what you need to do to realize your power and gift and protect your energy; it will just be something you know how to do and you will maintain your healthy life balance and sense of self. In contrast, you remain connected to others through your strong empathic senses.

The gifts of being an Empath have been shown to you throughout this book. Now all you need to do is follow through with the techniques and tools that will help you stay balanced, grounded, protected, and free of everyone else's emotional energy.

Grounding and Protection Meditation

The grounding and protection meditation will always come in handy. You can use it anywhere you are in as little as five minutes. Whenever you are feeling overwhelmed or like you are taking the brunt of someone's energetic pollution, you can step aside and find time to gift yourself some good grounding.

The power of a simple visualization and meditation is enough to help you regain balance and keep yourself in a healthier mental and emotional state. There will be plenty of times when it is not convenient to use this meditation. So you will have to resolve your imbalances with other tactics.

I find that the use of grounding and protective crystals and gemstones can be a very beneficial and useful tool. Hematite, onyx, tourmaline, obsidian, kyanite, and others are all very powerful grounding and protection stones that can be worn as jewelry or as an amulet. You can find a variety of crystals and stones at a local gem store or online. You can find a variety of other useful stones and crystals that are particularly useful for blocking energy and helping you restore your energy and emotions to a higher and more positive frequency.

Crystals and gemstones combined with the use of a grounding and protecting meditation will help you rekindle the personal balance you need to keep your Empathic abilities under control.

The Listening Bubble

Another method for grounding and protecting was mentioned as a useful tool for empathic and heartfelt listening. Still, it is also very powerful as energy to help you feel safe and protected from unwanted energy and emotional distress coming from other people.

Creative visualization is a powerful tool and has been scientifically proven to help people achieve their goals. Even famous Olympic athletes use visualization to win their gold medals. The more you practice, the easier it gets and the more detailed the imagery can be.

The Listening Bubble can also just be called "The Bubble". It can be used not only for practicing good listening but for using your energy in a better way. All you have to do is imagine yourself surrounded by a bubble of light that blocks out any unwanted energies. This can be most useful in one-on-one and group conversations, but can also be helpful if you are on an airplane and need energetic privacy, or if you are simply trying to feel protected and safe wherever you are.

I have even used "The Bubble" visualization around my car while driving down the highway because it made me feel safe and more protected from other drivers. I was better able to pay attention to where I was going and worried less about how other people were blasting down the highway.

It is a versatile tool and can be used in a variety of ways for a lot of different reasons. If you feel uncomfortable anywhere you are, in a conversation or even on the highway, build a bubble around yourself and allow it to protect you.

The Energy Magnet

The Energy Magnet is another useful visualization tool that can help you diffuse the emotional energy that is around you. Intense or extreme personalities that are loud and too close to you, or the unwanted emotions and distress of another, can all be sucked into the energy magnet.

You can picture it any way that feels easy for you. It could be a vacuum cleaner or an elephant whose trunk is sucking up all of the awkward energy. It could be an actual magnet that attracts the sensations you are feeling coming from someone else's person. Any way that you picture it, make sure it is something you can see well with your eyes open through your third eye.

Again, visualization can take practice and it can also be very fun. It is a unique way to help you redirect energy away from you and toward another idea or space in the room. You can play around with different ideas and images until you find the one that is your usual go-to image, and then keep it that way while you are at the office, handling job interviews, talking to an angry or upset customer, and more!

Affirmations of Empowerment

Affirmations are the key to a lot of people's success. Many CEOs and business elite use them as well as professional athletes and other successful public figures. Affirmations are an excellent way for you to focus your energy and power in new and different ways. They come in all shapes and sizes and are specific to your needs and desires.

In the other parts of this book gave several examples of affirmations that you can use to support your needs in dealing with the stress of other people's feelings and emotional pollution. It can be a creative process for you to have the affirmations of empowerment that work best for you for whatever situation you find yourself in.

You can create affirmations to relate to your relationships, your work environment, and coworker relationships, your friendships and family dynamics, everything! The point is that you allow yourself the proper language to help remain calm, balanced, and secure in your energy so that you are not taking on other people's energy and toxicity.

Affirmations are declarative statements and should be kept as simple as possible. Here are a few more examples to help you feel good about the different areas of your life that might need affirmations the most:

Workplace Affirmations

- I am capable of letting go of my work relationships at the end of the day.
- I am an empathic listener and I am also good at letting go of conversations when I need them to end.
- My gifts are an important part of how I do my job and I will continue to support them to the best of my ability.
- I can ground myself whenever I need to.
- I am good at protecting my energy around my coworkers.
- Friendships Affirmations
- I am a good friend and a good listener and I expect the same from my friends in return.
- I am understanding when the drama has to be discussed and I know when it is a good time to change the conversation to something more positive.
- I am available to all my friends in need when I can be.
- I would like to support my friends when I know that I can support my energy too.
- I know it is okay for me to say no to my friends when I need to take better care of myself today.

Family Affirmations

- I am connected and bonded to my family and I let them have their feelings and emotions that are different from mine.

- I am happiest when my family feels happy and sometimes I have to let them discover their happiness on their terms.

- I am good at spending time with my family and also seeking time for myself.

- I am connected to my relationships with my parents in new ways as myself and it keeps feeling better for me.

- I am proud of my ability to be an Empath for my family's needs and I want them to honor who I am and what my gifts are.

- Romantic Partnerships Affirmations

- I am capable of a healthy and balanced relationship and I want to see someone who is looking for the same, no matter what it takes.

- I am able to express myself well in my partnership when I am grounded and centered.

- I feel happiest when my relationships can let me be myself.

- I have to be supported by my partner as much as I support them.

- I will always take as good of care of myself as I do my romantic partners.

Sex Affirmations

- I am a sexual being and I feel things stronger than others.
- I can have casual love affairs as long as I know that is what we both are wanting.
- I am good at supporting my needs and the needs of others and can let go of my sexual partners when the time is right.
- I feel bonded and connected easily and can cut cords and move forward just as easily.
- Sexual communication is important to me and I value a communicative sexual partner.

All of these affirmations can help you take control of your energy and power. You can live the life you have always wanted without getting drained or exhausted by others when you use these simple and powerful tools regularly. There are so many others you can come up with on your own. Get creative and find the ones that will work best for you!

Energy Cleansing

Energy cleansing is a regular ritual. It can be done every day, multiple times a day and depending on how strong your Empath abilities are, you may need to try cleansing at least twice daily to start. Morning and night energy cleanses are my favorite and there are so many different possibilities for how it can be done.

You can use cleansing methods that you already know and trust, or try any of these methods below:

- Yoga
- Acupuncture
- Reiki
- Massage
- Chakra therapies
- Crystal and gemstone therapies
- Smudging (incense herb bundles)
- Walks in nature
- Hot, salty baths
- Meditation
- Creative visualization
- Painting
- Reading
- Listening to Music
- Dancing

There are certainly other ways that you may already know from your personal life. Create the routine of using energy clearing methods every day to help you stay in balance. The more you work to shift and release all of the emotional energy you collect throughout the day, the better and healthier you will feel.

The Waterfall

And finally, my favorite technique to block and absorb unwanted energies, the Waterfall visualization. Your eyes can see things without closing them. You can picture the idea of a stream of water floating between you and another person as you are speaking to them. Water is very calm and nurturing. It is the element of emotion. It allows you to stay open-hearted and loving. At the same time, you let other people's feelings pass into the flowing calm waters of your imagined waterfall.

This technique has worked for me so many times over the years and continues to do its job well.

11

Learn How to Handle Negative Energy to Support Yourself

Being an empath means that you are quite sensitive to the energies of those around you, places, and also nature. This sensitivity means that you tend to experience a rollercoaster of emotions. Therefore, it is important to learn about how protect yourself as an empath.

The wonderful gift of empathy can quickly turn into a nightmare if you don't know how to balance your energy or ground yourself. A lot of empaths develop addictions because they are absorbing too much energy from others and are unaware how they can protect themselves. By developing addictive behaviors, these empaths tend to numb themselves to all the energies around them and unconsciously try to protect their energy. However, this isn't the right way to go about it and will only harm you in the long run. Learning to balance your energies helps ensure that you are stable and are letting external energies harm you. It is about gaining stability, it helps heal yourself as an empath while healing others around you.

Protect Your Energy

Protecting yourself as an empath isn't something that must be taken lightly. If you do this, you will feel like the world is getting too complicated and troublesome. It will become impossible for you to cope with all the excess energy that you can feel. This, in turn, can effectively destroy any personal relationships that you have. By learning to protect and balance yourself, you get a chance to focus on what is most important to you. Protecting your energy is essentially about decluttering your life and ensuring that you aren't too vulnerable as an empath. In this part, you will learn about certain easy and practical steps you can follow to protect your energy as an empath.

Start Journaling

Start maintaining a journal to make a note of your feelings and the emotions you experience throughout the day. Journaling is a great way to reconnect with your innermost self. Also, when you make a note of your daily experiences, you can see the areas of your life where you need to improve yourself. It will give you a better insight into your nature and make you aware of your actions and reactions. Maybe there are instances where you wish you had reacted differently. Journaling gives you an opportunity for self-reflection. You can make a note of what you feel and how you wish you felt instead. You can also use it to write positive affirmations about yourself. This is essentially a technique to mentally and emotionally the clutter yourself from the challenges of life and stop you don't have to worry about whether what you're writing makes sense or not. Simply write about whatever you feel. It will give you better clarity. It is also an ideal technique for expelling any negative thoughts and emotions from your mind. Spend at least fifteen to 20 minutes at the end of the day to journalizing your experiences. It is a simple practice, and after a while, I'll become a habit. It is a conscious way to become self-aware.

Me time

Everyone needs to spend a little time by themselves. As an empath, you need this more than anyone else. You need some "me time" regardless of whether you have any other commitments to attend to or not. At times, the simplest means to recharge and protect your energy is by spending a little time with yourself. This is also an opportunity for self-reflection and self-care. Spend at least an hour by yourself every day. By distancing yourself physically from others, you can rejuvenate your body, mind, and soul. When you spend some time alone, all the energy that you will absorb from others will slowly disappear. If you are actively in contact with others' energies, you can concentrate on yourself. Spending time by yourself is unselfish, and you must not ignore it. You can meditate, spend some time writing in a journal, or engage in any other hobby that you like. Keep all your electronic gadgets away and concentrate on your energy.

Spending time outdoors

As an empathic healer, spending time in nature is the best way to recharge your energy. Whenever you get a chance, spend some time outdoors. You will feel more grounded and relaxed when you spend time in nature. You can sit under a tree, and maybe even meditate for a while. Visualize all the negative energy leaving your body. Picture it being absorbed by nature while you are absorbing nature's positivity. If you can, walk on grass for a while or even dip your feet in the water. Use the elements present in nature to heal your body and protect your energies. By walking barefoot, you can connect your energies with that of the ground or the Earth. It will help you stay grounded.

Take a Timeout

Remember that you are the only one who can control how you feel. You always have a choice, and you don't have to feel powerless. You'll feel powerless only when you give away this power to those. Things will affect you only if you let them. So, the best way to protect your energies is by taking a timeout. As an empath, it is only natural that you empathize with others, try to help them, or are upset or even judgmental of others' actions. This, in turn, creates a need within you to help others. Essentially, it means that you are trying to fix others regardless of whether they need any fixing or not. So, you are transferring your energy while absorbing theirs. Well, this merely means that you are shouldering their existing or perceived flaws as your own.

If you tend to do this, it is time to take a timeout. Start detaching yourself. No, you don't have to become a hermit. Instead, you must become selective about all the energies that you allow to enter you. You don't have to fix everyone else's problems, and it isn't your responsibility. It is okay to try and help others. However, you must not do this at great personal cost. Remember that every obstacle that you face in life is an opportunity to learn. If you don't learn your lesson, it is quite likely that you'll keep making the same mistake over and over again, and the lesson will continue to repeat itself in various situations until you learn from it. The same applies to others as well. So, by trying to fix them, you are depriving them of this opportunity to learn. Instead, make it a point to help them

when they come to you for help or advice. You don't have to
be a martyr.

Meditation

Meditation is an excellent way in which you can reconnect
with your true self. It helps you escape your everyday life and
look within yourself. Apart from this, meditation also makes
you more mindful and conscious of your thoughts, emotions,
and feelings. There are different ways in which you can
meditate. From practicing a simple breathing exercise to
devoting time for quiet self-reflection are all forms of
meditation. By practicing meditation, you can also calm your
mind and get mental clarity. We all lead rather stressful lives
these days, and empaths are under constant stress. By
meditating, you can quickly escape this stress and gain
equilibrium. Once you have mental clarity, it becomes easier to
concentrate on your daily activities.

To start meditating, close your eyes and try to visualize
your energy field. Once you do this, try to see any negative
energy, which is present in that field. Now, visualize that there
is a huge vacuum cleaner that's sucking out this negative energy.
Use this universal vacuum cleaner to get rid of any negativity
and protect your energies. As this vacuum removes all the
negative energy, visualize that it is being replaced with bright
white light or positive energy. This exercise takes only a couple
of minutes, and you can practice it whenever you want.

The best time to meditate is early in the morning when your mind is fresh. Try meditating outdoors for the best results. This not only helps you spend some time in nature but also revitalize your energy field and prepare yourself for the day ahead. Create a meditation routine for yourself and stick to the routine. Spending as little as 15 minutes every day meditating can bring about a positive change in your life. While meditating, ensure that you find a quiet spot to yourself without any distractions.

Sending It Back

When you spend some time and consciously think about it, you will realize that more than half the thoughts and emotions you're experiencing aren't your own. If something doesn't belong to you, return it. As an empath, your body acts like a sponge that absorbs every emotion or feeling that's present around it. To stop doing this, you must make a conscious decision to differentiate between your feelings and those of others. If you keep practicing that continuously and persistently, it becomes easier for you to make this distinction. If you notice any extreme emotion that you're experiencing isn't your own, send it back, with love and firm boundaries. It doesn't belong to you, so you must not allow it to affect you.

Energy Vampires

Whether you like to admit it or not, there will be people in your surroundings who tend to drain you of your energy. Even merely engaging in a conversation with such people will make you feel tired. Also, when others harbor any negative feelings or emotions about you, they unconsciously tend to send the same toward you. This negative energy being directed toward you while you're being drained of your positive energy will make you feel tired. Keep in mind that any intention that is emotionally charged is quite powerful. It doesn't matter whether this emotion is good or bad; it will have a direct effect on your energy field. The company you keep matters a lot. It tends to have a direct effect on how you feel.

Start spending time with people who make you feel better about yourself and who genuinely wish the best for you. If you notice that you feel tired after spending time with certain people, then it would be wise to stay away from them. Whenever possible, cut ties with all toxic people. If that's not possible, maintain as much distance from them as you physically can and limit your exposure to their toxic energies.

Water

Water represents the fluid energy of Earth, which washes away everything negative. The fluid nature of water helps cleanse your energy field. Cleansing yourself using water is a popular practice in various cultures across the world. You don't need holy water to do this. This is one of the reasons why people tend to feel calmer after taking a bath or shower. Stand under running water and notice how you feel better instantaneously. Or, you can even draw a warm bath with yourself and spend some time setting an art. You can infuse your bathwater with protective crystals or even your intentions for cleaning your energy. If you don't want to do this, then you can always visualize that you are allowing water to cleanse your energy field. Visualization is a very powerful tool, and when used wisely, it can help protect your energy field. Visualize that as the water runs down your body, it is taking away every ounce of negative energy that surrounds you.

Shield Yourself

There is a simple shielding technique you can use to protect yourself from negativity. Visualize that you are surrounded by a cocoon or a protective cloak around your physical body. Essentially, you must visualize some sort of shape around your body, which will act as a shield. The next step is to visualize that there is a small opening in this shield either at the top of your head or below your feet.

12

Understanding Psychic Empaths

There are different kinds of empaths who specialize in specific types of psychic work. Geomancy is a skill in which the empath senses the energies and vibrations of the earth. You can use this skill in dousing, detecting water underground, or predicting upcoming bad weather. Psychometry is the psychic ability, which enables an empath to obtain impressions from various objects. This is sometimes used by the police in solving strange or violent crimes.

Clair cognizance is another unique skill in which the empath knows exactly what measures to take or actions to perform in any given situation, especially during an emergency or a crisis. They can act with self-assurance, peace and calmness, inspiring everyone around them to act in the same way.

Some empaths can also sense spirits and work with them, a psychic ability called mediumship. Some can heal by feeling other people's symptoms and help them by transmuting energies. Similarly, they can help others overcome emotional traumas. Some empaths can communicate with nature in general while others do the same with animals. Precognition is another rare gift in which psychic empaths can perceive events or disasters that are about to occur.

While empaths are endowed with significant abilities as mentioned above, they often pay a high price for these. Often, they are being judged and misunderstood. Sometimes, they also receive derogative, even contemptuous, remarks for their declarations. Empaths can be particularly sensitive of their environment, causing them to acquire physical up-sets and strange allergies that cannot be diagnosed by regular medical practitioners.

Although their talents and abilities are truly significant, they are not all-knowing. Their skills may not work at optimum levels all the time, nor can they heal all ills and diseases of humankind.

History of Psychic Empaths

Since prehistoric times, psychics played a notable role in human culture. They often hold positions as priests, priestesses, seers and mystics in various religions before the inception of Christianity.

Many psychic seers can be found in the Bible, including Samuel, Gad and Amos. Samuel was the one who found the donkey of King Saul. Gad was King David's seer, while Amos was the seer commanded by Amaziah to escape Judah and practice his prophetic endeavors outside that land.

One of the most recognized names in ancient psychics is the Greek Oracle of Delphi. It wasn't an actual person, but rather an office convened by the cleverest woman in Delphi. She interpreted information directly from Apollo, the God of Light and Truth. Her visions were increased by the natural steams emanating from the hot springs in the Delphi area. In ancient Egypt, the well-known seers were the priests of Ra on Memphis. In Assyria, oracles were called nabu, meaning "announce" or "to call."

During the Renaissance period in France, Nostradamus became a famous name in prophesying. His prophesies are still well-recognized across the globe and have been on print consistently since they were first written.

In mid-1800s, when the planet Neptune was discovered (a discovery that rules psychics), the Spiritualist Movement began and expanded. Many psychics flourished during that period, including Edgar Cayce, Daniel Dunglas Home, and Madame Blavatsky.

Psychic empaths have walked the Earth ever since the dawning of humankind's history. However, it was only during the New Age Awakening of the 70s and 80s that empathic skills were recognized as being distinct from other psychics.

How Empaths Feel

Since empaths are highly sensitive to the different energies surrounding them, they often fall victim to inner conflict and tremendous stress. When an empath's empathetic nature is in full effect, he may experience abnormal nervousness or feel as if an electrical current is suddenly overpowering him. This is followed by an overflow of emotions.

Strong melancholic feelings may arise out of nowhere and engulf him. This can become confusing for the empath since he may not completely understand what's happening to him. He takes on those feelings as his own and tries to formulate an explanation as to why he feels such unfounded emotions.

Because of this, it is no surprise that most empaths become depressed at some point of their life. Depression may even be a recurring visitor for many of them. Besides negative emotions, empaths can also absorb other people's positive vibrations. However, this up-and-down phenomenon can create an emotional rollercoaster ride for the untrained, unaware and inexperienced empath.

How Empaths Obtain Information

The true mechanisms of psychic/empathic abilities are still unknown. Numerous theories have been made in an attempt to explain such mechanisms. Still, all of it were mere matters of conjecture. Not all empaths possess only one ability. Some can obtain information using multiple psychic skills that work in unison to create one "mega" psychic ability.

For instance, an empath may use his psychometric abilities to obtain information by simply touching a person or an object. Then, his empathic ability processes that information to induce feelings. Looking beyond those two psychic abilities, the empath may also possess strong clairaudience, clairvoyance, and other skills that facilitate the processing of all the information he is receiving.

It can be difficult for a psychic empath to find ways to control the information he receives until he stops to evaluate his processes and determine if he is operating only on empathic abilities or a set of abilities. Testing oneself on each potential ability requires a great deal of patience and time. However, once the empath has successfully established a baseline, it will be much easier to comprehend how his psychic ability is related and how his combined abilities function and interact.

Opening Up Your Inner Abilities

If you have gone through all of the contained in this, you will know that you need to go through the pages again to fulfill your wish to become a psychic. However, we thought that putting the blueprint here in one would help you to make a list of the things that you need to do to move forward in this venture.

Take up Meditation - The sooner you do this the better. If you want meditation to make a difference, you can do no better than simply going on a retreat where trained gurus will be able to guide you. I would suggest that professional help is better than trying to go the road alone because you will need to learn new systems of thought that will help you to achieve the best that you can from your meditative practice. The problem with trying to do this on your own is that you may be missing out on a real opportunity to learn all about what's going on inside you. Many try to meditate alone and give up because they don't get past the initial tries and find that it's too hard to concentrate. However, in a retreat, you will learn the benefit of taking this seriously and it will help you to open up the intuitive side of your character which is where all of your psychic abilities are located.

Learn about Chakras - The reason you need to learn this is so that you can instantly recognize the problems that your clients have without there being too much verbal interaction. If you understand the power of the Chakras, you are better equipped to help those who seek your assistance.

Spend time in natural surroundings – This helps you to quieten the mind. To be a good psychic you need to be in this moment in your life. If you are too busy in the world of commercialism you forget about the way that nature nurtures. That's very important. It helps you to be empathetic and it helps you to be at one with yourself which is vital for anyone who is going to give any kind of spiritual guidance to others.

Practice Clairvoyance in your everyday life – You may wonder how you can do this. Clairvoyance simply means "clear seeing." That means that you must not complicate your life and that you need to go back to basics. Clairvoyance has absolutely nothing to do with seeing into the future. It simply means being able to visualize. This is a very necessary skill to a psychic and practicing visualization is important. To do this, close your eyes and look. Try to think of something that makes you feel happy and prosperous and hone in on the vision. See it. Feel it and most of all live it. This will help you with your clarity of purpose and will sustain you when you make errors of judgement. You cannot always be right, but you can learn by visualization to use the times when you are wrong as lessons so that in the future, your predictions and readings are more accurate.

Learn to become grounded - As we have explained in, life is made up of energies. Those who are not grounded are more likely to dwell in the past or worry about the future. When you do yoga, for example, your hands are given a particular position to keep you grounded during your yoga practice. If you are not practicing yoga, you need to find that balance within yourself.

Practice with Psychometry – Often used for criminal investigations, this form of psychic energy is when you hold an object in your hand and take the vibration sent from that object to tell you something about the owner of the object. It can be a piece of jewelry, or a set of keys or even a garment that has the aroma of an individual still on it – rather than fresh out of the washing machine. Close your eyes and rub the object in your hand until you feel all the energy flowing from the object into your hands. You can start by asking yourself simple questions such as whether the owner is a woman or a child. You can also ask yourself how old this person is. Write down your responses and then check up on their accuracy. You may find that you are more gifted than you thought.

Memory recall – This is vital and helps you to develop your fundamental skills. Have a friend place five objects onto a tray in front of you. You have several moments to look at them and to associate them with your friend. Then the tray is taken away and you need to recall as much detail as you can about the items. This is valuable because it makes you more observant.

Seeking things out - Hold an object in your hand and pass it to a friend. Ask your friend to hide the item in your home and then use your instincts to find it. Try to hone in on the vibrations of the item because this helps you to develop your psychic skills.

Practice Telepathy – Ask a friend to help you with this exercise. Take four numbers and ask them to concentrate on one of them. Ask them to take this seriously and to try to transmit to you the number that they are thinking about. Close your eyes and take the energy of their thoughts into your mind to guess what the number is. This same game can be used with colors, shapes, objects etc. to help you to build up your ability to telepathically work out the message your friend is trying to pass to you.

Learning to sense energy fields - If you have classes near you where energy is explored, then these are ideal for learning all about taking in the energy from people around you and also learning about auras. These help you to release your own energy and to correct the flow so that you are able to see clearly what it is that you need to address. People with blocked energy often find that their psychic abilities are also blocked because of this. If you need to be assured about the importance of the energy flow, look at the on Chakras.

13

Benefits and Challenges of Empathy

Simply put, an empath is a person with heightened sensory awareness who experiences the emotions of others. They easily attune to the feelings of those around them by interpreting body language, and can gauge the emotions of others by observing subtle facial gestures, called micro expressions, that reveal fleeting feelings of disgust, fear, happiness, sadness, or contempt. They are also adept at interpreting hand gestures or facial expressions. Through intuition and instinctual observation, an empath can feel someone else's emotions with intensity.

What Does It Mean to Be an Empath?

For an empath, attunement is a reflex. Empaths go about their daily lives, picking up and processing emotions along the way like a magnet. Because of this ability, empaths need intentional self-care and deliberate management of their emotions to avoid overwhelm (which occurs from exposure to too much stimulus), anxiety, and depression.

While a robust empathic nature is indeed a gift, regular exposure to others' emotions can quickly lead to depletion, exhaustion, and feelings of imbalance. Knowing how to manage daily experiences and interactions properly is critical. By using mindfulness techniques and the tools in this book, empaths can protect their well-being and ease the anxiety that accompanies them wherever they go.

Similarities and Differences Between Introverts and Empaths

Empaths and introverts are similar in many ways, but there are some subtle distinctions between them. For instance, both empaths and introverts need alone time to reenergize and regain their sense of peace at the end of the day. The critical difference is that an empath also uses this alone time to shake off the emotions collected from other people throughout the day, whereas introverts simply need to recharge and don't necessarily need to process emotions they've accrued from others. A common misconception is that all empaths are introverts. While many empaths are introverted, there are plenty of extroverted, and even ambiverts, empaths who all reenergize in different ways.

The real magic emerges for empaths, whether an introvert or an extrovert, when they learn to tap into their unique empathic nature, develop their empathic strengths, and combine these strengths with emotional-processing skills to create an integrated balance that allows them to thrive. Empaths have the ability to give challenging experiences meaning by engaging in transformational actions for reducing anxiety and managing emotional well-being.

Empath Children

Children are masters of attunement, and they learn how to navigate their emotional landscape from their adult caregivers. Infants instinctually align their heartbeat to match their mother's while breastfeeding, cuddling, or sleeping. Through this alignment, children grow and evolve by attuning to their caregiver to satisfy their practical needs for food, sleep, and affection. Likewise, they also attune to their adult caregivers to satisfy their emotional needs. By learning how to attune, their attachment style emerges. If the caregiver is distant or dissociated, an infant will show distress and emotional confusion while trying to attune because they are so desperate to establish a connection that makes them feel safe. When an infant experiences an engaged parent who is connected to their emotions and mentally present, it's more likely the infant will develop a secure attachment.

Empath children are no different in their need to connect to their caregiver but may require less stimulation to maintain emotional balance. Bright lights, loud voices, or chaotic family systems are engaging for many children, but for an empath child, this stimulation can be overwhelming and their need to attune to a parent for emotional comfort will become evident. While all infants rely on their caregivers to calm their unregulated moods, highly sensitive children might need parental soothing more often because they experience states of overstimulation frequently. Additionally, highly sensitive and empathic children might display an exaggerated reaction to sensory stimulation compared to other children.

Self-soothing is an essential skill that empathic children need in order to cope with the drama of daily living, sensory overload, and emotional overwhelm. A caregiver can support a highly sensitive child by patiently observing the ways the child naturally exhibits self-soothing behaviors and encouraging the child to develop routines that engage those behaviors. Caregivers can be supportive by providing a comforting presence while an overwhelmed child expresses their emotions and can also use calm breathing to soothe a distressed child. Helping a child soothe lays a foundation for the child's future ability to self-soothe.

Empath Parents

Part of the parenting experience is a deep sense of empathy for our children while supporting them as they explore complex and challenging emotions. Empathic parents need to balance their own emotions while sensing the emotional landscapes of their children. Learning to establish and maintain ethical boundaries is a crucial tool for doing the emotional labor that supports the family. Empathic parents will feel the emotions of their children, but it doesn't have to be at the expense of their own well-being. In fact, it's imperative to find ways to self-soothe, practice self-care, and develop good emotional hygiene in order to create a foundation of harmony in the home. Remember that children attune to their caregivers and are subconsciously looking at them to know how to feel and how to develop their emotional language. Tending to your emotional health as an empath will teach your children to do the same and increase their emotional intelligence.

An empath parent has a deep well of emotional resources to offer the family. An Animal Empath can teach children how to show loving kindness to animals and inspire a lifelong relationship of caring for sentient beings and the fulfillment that such care brings. An Intuitive Empath can use all five senses to bring worlds of curiosity and wonder to their children and help them hone their own developing senses. Empath parents can also use their empathic nature to decide how to spend quality time with their children. Aesthetic Empaths can visit a museum with their kids and connect over the shared sensory experience of viewing a work of art. Likewise, Physical Empaths can bond with their children through sports, yoga, or other physical activities.

Parents often want to be perceived as perfect caretakers who have endless patience to nurture their child through their struggles gently. Realistically, parents feel insecure about their parenting ability more often than not, because they don't know if the choices they're making are right or wrong. They are imperfectly doing their best.

Being a parent is challenging no matter what. But the desire for a deep level of love and connection leads people to want to become parents in the first place. For all the rewarding, oxytocin-induced bonding parents do with their kids, there are moments of exhaustion, frustration, and soul-deep depletion. Kids are loud, messy, stubborn, expensive, and often inexhaustible. All these things have the potential to rock an empath to their core.

Additionally, the culture of raising children is more intense now than it has ever been. Daycare, spirituality choices, education, and expectations around nutrition leave parents feeling judged and diminished. Relying on empathic strengths to bolster parenting skills is a powerful tool for self-support and guidance that's being adopted by the communities that make up the proverbial "village" we need to raise lovely, integrated humans.

RED As an Emotional Empath, you can assess which emotions belong to you and which belong to someone else by asking yourself two questions.

First, "What was I feeling right before I became angry (or sad or activated)?" Second, "Was there a triggering event that preceded this feeling?" If you were feeling fine, and there wasn't an easily identifiable trigger, chances are you picked up someone else's emotion. Ground yourself with a few deep breaths and allow the feeling to pass.

INDIGO As an Animal Empath, you understand that animals have their own ways of communicating and that not all animals want to be touched.

You can sense when a dog is feeling protective, scared, or unpredictable. Verbalize these vital signals to children so they develop a respectful relationship with animals. When a dog has its tail down and lips curled, it's probably best to observe them from afar. Your child's intent for wanting to engage with animals is probably just to grab a quick cuddle, but things can quickly turn harmful for both animals and children if the complex behaviors of animals are ignored. Your secure connection with animals is something to share with your kids so they learn to respect these subtle cues, too.

VIOLET As an Intuitive Empath, you have mastery over the sensory information you receive.

You've learned the hard way what happens when you talk yourself out of what you know and fail to trust your gut. Remember a time when you went against your intuition and the adverse repercussions that occurred. Journal about the experience and then tune in to how you feel in your body. Write down any feelings that arise. Unpacking the experience through journaling gives it meaning and deepens your emotional wisdom. Keep this journal entry as a resource and refer to it whenever you find yourself doubting your instincts as a parent.

14

Fundamentals of Psychic Training

Psychic Training Guidelines

You will begin to evolve and change once you step into the supernatural world. You will experience the world as you've never seen it before. When heading into unknown territory, we must be prepared with the right tools. The experience can be a little overwhelming and sometimes disorienting. If you are not focused, it will all be a waste of time. Following are some basic guidelines to enhance your psychic abilities.

The Right Attitude

With practice, you will become more adept and natural with your natural psychic gift. It will eventually become merely another part of you. You are not just an extension of a psychic ability, you embody it. It's how you are able to say that you have psychic ability. Once you master your abilities, you will be a psychic. As your development grows, it will become a way of life. You become a psychic by actively seeking it.

As with any other skill, some people are born with it while others develop it with practice. It becomes a part of who they are. The gift is not feared; therefore, it is like a natural part of them. With time, others will be able to awaken their psychic ability. If this is you, you may have to work at it harder but you will still be able to harness that power. The key to developing psychic potential is a willingness to trust and know that it's there. Listen to your inner voice even if it goes against everything you have been taught your whole life. You must open your mind and be willing to let go of traditional ideas and embrace a whole new world.

If it seems too hard at first and you feel like you are getting nowhere, keep trying and trust your potential. Consistency is essential. If you are not consistent, you are not going to see results. It's going to take you longer to harness your power. You can't rush through things. If you do, you will find yourself discouraged and even frightened by what is being revealed to you. Patience is the key. It will guide you and keep you moving at a pace that will help you become an effective psychic.

Better Memory

If you don't get the right amount of sleep, you are not going to use your intuition to its fullest. To work at maximum capacity, your mind needs rest. The dreams or visions you have while sleeping may be something you must remember to follow your intuition. Keeping records of your dreams might help you locate a pattern. Patterns are useful in getting a full picture of what your mind is thinking. Buddhist monks meditate to reach Nirvana. This simply means that they are trying to reach inner wisdom that everyday life can't give them. Total concentration in meditation must happen to get anything from meditation. Sleep is another way to get inside your head and see things more clearly. Try to get at least eight hours a night and have a journal handy to jot down your dreams. Just like your body is healing itself during sleep, your mind is sorting through your problems. Recording your dreams in a diary while they are fresh in your mind will give you greater insight, which will help you develop your intuition.

By recording your dreams, you will start trusting what you find coming from your subconscious. This is important while developing your abilities.

Respect Your Psychic Skill

By accessing your psychic skills, you are diving into a whole new world, one that holds large amounts of power. Misusing this power can bring trouble into your life. Using power beyond your ability will attract the wrong attention. You could also cause harm to befall others as well as hurt the reputation of psychics in general. Don't overstate, boast, or try to set yourself up as Miss So and So. You're not in this to start a hotline. You do this to use a gift you've been able to develop and share with others.

To quote Spiderman's uncle, "With great power comes great responsibility." It's best to adapt as you journey through this realm. Proceed with honesty and integrity for yourself, others, and your gift. You shouldn't try to share your ability with others until you are confident in it. As you enter this realm, you might feel uncomfortable or unhinged at times. That's perfectly normal. It's all part of the process. The more you accept the beautiful new things coming your way, the easier the transition.

This journey will open you up to becoming more sensitive to all the subtle things in the world. You may start to see things that make you think you are hallucinating, for example, shadow figures in your peripheral vision, lights, or auras. You may hear things that don't seem to come from anywhere or experience other phenomena. Anything is possible. As you become more open, you may start to sense a presence or someone close to you.

There's no need to be afraid. These things have always been there. You have simply become more aware of them. You must adjust to these things over time. They will soon become a part of who you are and your everyday life. You will soon have a bunch of new friends.

The Sixth Sense is a movie that portrays a little boy who sees dead people. He is frightened by his ability because he doesn't understand what is happening to him. His mother thinks he is disturbed and hires a psychologist to help him understand his ability. Over time, the psychologist helps him accept his gift of "sixth sense." This example reminds us that not everyone will accept the ability to see things that others can't. Take care when telling others about your visions because they might not be ready to share your experiences. You could also end up damaging your relationship with them if they are not understanding of these kinds of things.

You must be able to take disappointments because your other sense might let you down. You might make a mistake when reading someone's future or even coming up with ideas about their past. Embrace humility. This helps you see mistakes as a learning curve that helps you move beyond normal limitations. Sure, you will make mistakes but don't let it allow you to stop trusting yourself. You attempted to come up with answers for someone and you should look at it as such. You are going to encounter surprises along the way; just learn from them. The most significant learning aid is experimenting with your psychic ability.

Stay Grounded

As your awareness of the subtleties of reality increase, you could start to feel detached from the physical world. You could think of it as daydreaming. You stay loosely attached to everyday life while exploring higher and deeper realms of imagination. It's good that you have opened yourself up to an enhanced reality. To maintain a healthy life while using your psychic gifts, you must learn to merge the two into your everyday existence.

This is why you must bring your awareness from the conscious mind more in-depth into the other states of consciousness, rather than the other way around. If you only open yourself to the higher states, you might start to lose your grip on reality. You might experience imbalance and have a loss of psychological equilibrium. In extreme cases, this concept occurs in people who have schizophrenia. They might be tuned into elements beyond our reality but they don't understand what's happening. They are caught in their own world and can't establish a balance between it and the physical world. This detachment creates a psychological split. People with schizophrenia are unable to distinguish between a supernatural world and a physical world. They have lost the ability to accept the right place of either in their lives.

Not staying grounded may affect your ability to remain organized, to follow and contribute to logical conversation, or to manage your time well. It can become more challenging to maintain the essential functions of the physical world because you are becoming detached from them. You must incorporate all aspects of life and integrate them into a holistic balance by opening yourself up while staying active and organized on a practical level. You will have a much smoother journey when you can stay grounded throughout the process.

How do you stay grounded? Stay up to date with your everyday tasks. Sit on the ground. This connects you to the Earth and the physical world by synchronizing your energy with the grounded frequencies of the Earth. Get out in nature. Walking ten minutes each day will do wonders for your mental and emotional states. Metal such as copper and individual crystals will help keep you balanced.

When you stay grounded, you help develop a foundation from which you can go through the higher realms of consciousness confidently without getting swept away. Think about a pyramid. The base is your foundation, keeping you connected with the Earth. As you climb the pyramid, the structure melds, culminating in the totality at the pyramid's pinnacle. This is your acute clarity of mind, able to connect with any frequency in the universe, to be of excellent service to the world, and to access vast amounts of knowledge.

Yoga or meditation is a great way to stay grounded, as these practices help you look within rather than be influenced by the world around you. When we look at people, we assume things. The world is made up of assumptions based on modern beliefs. Look beyond them; don't judge a book by its cover. Learning inner focus through yoga or meditation will keep you grounded so you can see your skills in another light.

The problem with society is that we forget what being grounded means. It has nothing to do with fitting in. Nor does it mean we must act in a certain way. It simply means being able to focus one's thoughts and pick up the vibrations which help us use our abilities. You simply trust your inner instincts. A great deal of observation is used when you demonstrate your psychic abilities. This can be seen in the character Patrick Jane on the TV show "The Mentalist". This character has worked at being a psychic in the past. He owes his ability to being grounded and being able to see things other people may not. His observation ability is astounding. This shows us that even though he is a fictional character, the fact that he can remain grounded is the most essential part of his ability.

Grounding simply means believing in oneself. Once achieved, you can demonstrate your psychic ability in much better ways. Sureness and clarity are very important because they will help you develop your intuition. Instead of starting with preconceived ideas and morals, grounding allows you to start from the beginning. You will find that you are more grounded and able to deal with problems rationally when you take judgment out of the picture. You can listen to people and help them work out their problems without letting judgment get in the way of your psychic ability. Grounding merely means having a base upon which to start your session. This is the you that you were as a child—not worrying about anything. It's the you that shows up when you sleep. Its needs are uncomplicated and allow you to look beyond the problem to see what lies beneath.

Just like D. Takara Shelor said, "The more you meditate, spend time in nature, raise your consciousness, and get in touch with the more spiritual side of life, the more highly refined and sensitive you will become to subtle energy."

15

The Qualities of Psychic Empathy

You Are Aware of Everything Around and In You

The average person is often aware of what is going on in their life, at least to a reasonable extent. They can tell what they are thinking about, they are peripherally aware of what is happening in their external environment, and they are able to read the verbal and visual cues from the people they are surrounded by. A psychic empath takes this a notch higher. They can sense just about everything in themselves and their external environment. They are able to walk in a room and immediately read the mood of the room. They can tell when a person is getting angry or upset even before it shows on their face. If you are a psychic empath, you will find yourself being very aware of what is happening in your life and even in the lives of the people you care about. If a friend is going through a heartbreak, you will share their pain in a way that others cannot, even before your friend makes this pain public knowledge.

You Hate Crowds and Prefer Being Alone

While you care a lot about people, you also prefer to interact with them on a one-on-one basis and not while they are in a crowd. You find crowds overwhelming and prefer to keep your own company. You like solitude because it allows you to recharge your energy. You cannot survive for long in a crowd setting. Crowds steal your joy; they make you nervous and anxious and they drain you. The reason why crowds drain you so quickly is because you are continually picking up energy signals from people and being in a crowd means you are bombarded with so many signals that you get overwhelmed. Do you prefer staying indoors to going out? Are you the kind of person who would rather watch a concert on TV than actually attend the concert in person?

You Are an Amazing Listener

A downside of being known as a good listener is that people tend to take that as their cue to dump all their problems on you. If you have been suspecting all along that you are an empath, this is a problem that you likely have. Empaths are often keen to understand people truly and they do this by listening more than they talk. People love good listeners. Most people love talking about themselves and will gravitate towards anyone who gives them the chance. Because of your excellent listening abilities, you may have found yourself playing therapist to friends and strangers alike. Unfortunately for you, you might not have a whole lot of empaths in your life who return the favor. The journal you write in every night before you go to bed might be the only listening ear that you turn to after you have spent your entire day listening to other people rant about everything and anything.

You Are Highly Emotional and Often Moody

An empath feels their emotions and then feels other people's emotions. Naturally, there is going to be a whole lot of moodiness going on. Imagine having to deal with the emotions of six people within an hour. How would that make you feel? Moody, at best and murderous at worst. This is the daily predicament of an empath. They may leave their house feeling all happy and content only to experience six different emotions even before they get to work. If you have a person in your life who seems to have a new emotion every hour, it might be that they are an empath whose feelings are linking with the emotions of other people.

You Often Feel Emotionally and Mentally Drained

As a psychic empath, it is natural to feel depleted at the end of the day when you have used up all the emotional, mental, and physical resources that are available to you. It can be especially daunting if you are working in a situation where you are regularly exposed to people who are in pain or who are upset. What makes it worse is that there are people who consciously drain your energy from you once they figure out that you are an empath. These people are referred to as energy vampires. elves into the details of how to identify an energy vampire on top of sharing some simple tactics that you can employ to protect yourself when faced with an energy vampire.

Kids and Animals Naturally Gravitate Towards You

Kids and pets are not known to be articulate as far as communicating other people's intentions. However, they are both extremely intuitive. What young children and animals lack in communication skills they make up for in intuition. Intuition is defined as the ability to understand instinctively without relying on conscious reasoning. What this means is that a child will instinctively know that you are a right person without going through the steps of logical reasoning. The same case applies to pets. If you are the person that the dog runs to every time even though there are other people in the room, then maybe you need to start looking at yourself more differently. Mainly if the other signs of the psychic empath as listed above already apply to you.

You Struggle with Intimate Relationships

As an empath; it is common to struggle with the need to be loved while also wanting to be alone. Togetherness may not be your cup of tea, especially when this togetherness means being overloaded daily. Psychic empaths have to go through a wide range of emotions as they interact with people daily. When they are given a choice to be in a relationship or not, many psychic empaths want the opportunity to be alone just because it's so much easier than being with someone. It's not that they want to be alone forever; it's just that they have gone through the motions of being emotionally drained and they just don't feel like going through it again. It can be quite the delicate balancing act, and many times you will find yourself pushing people away. Some people may assume that you are simply scared of commitment without realizing that you are healing yourself from emotional scars and do not want to take any more on board.

Spirituality Resonates with You

There are many different religions in the world with all sorts of rules and ideologies. However, all these strict rules of what you can and cannot do just don't make sense to you. When someone who is gifted with great intuition, they instinctively know what is morally right and wrong and abide their own natural laws that feel right to them. In today's world, the only concept that seems to make sense to the empath is spirituality. Spirituality is a comprehensive concept, giving the empath a sense of freedom, encouraging a path of self-discovery, growth, and connectedness.

Spirituality also expresses the notion that we are a part of something much bigger than this just this physical world. We are not a human having a physical experience. We are in fact, an eternal soul having a human experience. And this resonates well for the Empath as it ties in with their higher purpose of helping people in the physical world and increasing the Earth consciousness.

You Love Connecting with Nature

Granted, many people love to admire the beauty of the natural world. For you, though, the connection feels more profound and more personal. You love to steal moments at the park, and your ideal home would be a cabin in the woods surrounded by the sights and sounds of the wild. Nature replenishes your energy. You love the greenery of trees, the ocean, and you love to spend your time hiking in the trails. You are never unhappy when you are out and about exploring the natural wonders of the Universe. After getting your energy sapped by those around you, you love the comfort of knowing that nature can restore this energy to the last bit.

You Have Been Accused of Being Too Nice

Empaths really do have hearts of gold. The problem with this is that they do not know when to stop pouring into others. If you are a psychic empath that will give the last shirt on your back, you probably have a few good friends who have picked up on the same. These are the friends who will accuse you of being too sweet and tell you that you need to stop giving too much to people because they can see how much it drains you. What your friends may not know is that your generosity is ingrained in your DNA.

You Have a Very Active Mind

Most Empaths are quite introverted, which means they are in their head a lot. Thinking, observing, daydreaming, visualizing, reflecting and creating. Empaths view the world entirely different to the average person. This with their gifted intuition, comes a significant edge, to create many amazing things to impact the world significantly.

However, this is usually restricted, especially in the empaths early journey from things such as lack of confidence, low self- worth, fear, doubt and uncertainty. Over time as the empath listens to their intuition and focuses on ridding these low vibrational qualities, life becomes exciting.

Struggles of an Empath

As an empath, you will likely have struggled that non-empaths cannot identify with. Simple situations that non-empaths can quickly deal with (because they aren't using a whole lot of their emotional resources) will quickly drain you and leave you feeling overwhelmed. Empaths often find themselves struggling on a daily basis, and it can be even harder when you do not already know that you are an empath. As such, you might find yourself questioning why you tend to react in a particular manner when the people around you seem to take everything in their stride.

Mainstream Media Is Overwhelming and Draining

While most people look at television as a form of entertainment and a means to unwind after a long day, empaths often have quite the opposite outlook. Television shows can be exceptionally draining for an empath because of the myriad of emotions that producers and directors are aiming to elicit out of their audience. What's more, the news has turned into somewhat of a horror show in itself. Whether news anchors are reporting about the latest Middle East crisis or looming wars between dissenting countries, it only takes minutes before the empath starts their downward spiral into unpleasant emotions.

Empaths Don't Like Saying No

Empaths also often struggle with saying no to others. Most people, empaths or not, do not like to say no to others. There is an individual struggle that comes with denying someone what they want, even when you know it's for the best. It is not for nothing that there are campaigns aimed at helping others know that "no" is a complete statement and answer on its own. When you say no to a person's request, there are often negative feelings that will come by as a result. There might be guilt and even resentment. Empaths hate dealing with negative feelings. They prefer to say "yes" because they like to make other people happy. At the same time, they do not want to deal with any negative emotions that might result from turning down a person's request because then they might be drained by these negative emotions. At the end of the day, empaths find themselves in a rather tricky position where they need to learn to create boundaries by saying no but also protect their energy by learning how to say no in the most tactful way possible.

Empaths Struggle with Crowds and Group Interactions

Imagine being able to pick up people's energies just by being in their presence. How would that make you feel? For a moment, it might be fun knowing that you can read someone without even needing to ask what they are feeling.

16

How to Prevent Empathic Pain

Life can be a collection of anxieties, hurts, pain, and the list goes on. Many people, especially adults, carry emotional baggage. Empaths are able to collect these energies whether they like it or not. Energy transfer among people is entirely natural, but sometimes someone sends their energy in an unpleasant way.

While there are many empaths in this world, there are also many energy vampires. Some people might be unaware as well that they are vampires, but the dangerous ones are those who are aware on the ways to suck out energies from others. They can also release negative energies. Since empaths strongly absorb energies, they become the target of these vampires.

Empaths can also fall victim to toxic people who dump their emotional garbage on other people. Empaths are also natural givers and that is why energy vampires target them often as prey.

Vampires are the opposite of empaths in that they are takers. They crave attention and praise. These vampires are also called narcissist. They don't genuinely care about others but themselves. Once the attention and praises stop coming, they will be very irritable and aggressive. They will be cruel and punishing, controlling the empath to feed more energy to them.

Since these vampires can be so seductive at first, an empath may find hope that they will change someday, but they won't. They will just keep on harassing other people and bringing them into their sick cycle of seduction and coercion. The best way to overcome these vampires is by totally cutting them off. Block them. There is no need to try to change them or hope in them.

Energy vampires also thrive in chaos. Even in good times, they manage to find something negative about it and blow it out of proportions. They make a big deal out of small hitches and make a hysteria out of it. They can be like drama queens who always crave the attention of others and will create all sorts of scandalous scenarios (especially in public) to shame other people.

Empaths should remain calm during these moments. They should not pander to the crises created by energy vampires. Breathing deeply and releasing tension helps an empath to calm down and recover their center. Breathing clears the head of the menagerie of instantaneous reactions and gives way for a more focused solution. It will be tough to sway an empath who is grounded and centered.

Even if empaths have a way of giving and nurturing others by helping them ease their pain, it's not right to abuse them and make them on-call personal therapists. An empath should realize when other people are taking advantage of depleting their seemingly always-available stores of energy. No matter how difficult, setting or limiting boundaries should be enforced by an empath.

Yoga is one of the proven ways to strengthen a person's core. A strong core results in mindfulness and heightened awareness of one's power. Through constant yoga practice, and empath becomes more potent in deflecting demands made by pain-inflicting persons. They can monitor their stores of energy and direct their focus on restorative aims.

Deep breathing and humming help an empath to regain lost energy. Humming is a form of vocalization that creates a vibration that communicates and harmonizes with cosmic energies. It is a way of releasing energies to the vastness of the cosmos.

Empaths naturally have fragile emotional skins. That's why it is oftentimes easily invaded. Sadly, it is only in hindsight that an empath is able to assess a situation when their skins were breached. They look back and judge what happened and how their fortress failed at one point.

Once they are able to assess what happened, they can change their filter settings accordingly so that they can make better quick-thinking decisions in the future. It's very much liked the physical body's auto-immune system which, after getting attacked by a particular virus, develops the needed protectors and strengthening agents in a continuously-evolving process. The next time an empath comes across a similar situation, he can say, "Oh, I've seen this before. I know what I can do about it."

For an empath, these attacks may seem like a never-ending challenge. However, it is actually a natural process of spiritual evolution. It integrates an empath's nervous system and filters so that they can discern situations better in the future. There may be pain still, but it is lessened because of the level of anticipation and recognition of a potentially painful situation. It's a learning process.

Sometimes, pain is inflicted on an empath because he or she is rejected by the society. This may be because of the powers he or she possesses. Even friends and relatives can be cruel when faced with something they do not understand. That is human nature. Rejection and isolation can cause depression and anxieties in an empath. They may build walls that are as high as the sky to prevent further pain.

Rather than escape the pain, an empath must go into the pain. There is no use trying to escape. It is better to confront the pain that will give way to proceeding to the next step in healing the hurts. It can help to go to genuine healers and they can guide you in the healing process. Ultimately, the efforts should come from you.

While you can prevent some pains, there are also sudden attacks. This can lead to a flood of emotions. It is helpful for an empath to practice body-mindfulness. You must teach yourself to get in touch with your body. Cry or laugh as you feel you must. Listen to your needs. Repression of your own emotions will only lead to further confusion and a build-up of negative emotions.

As an empath, you must learn to love yourself. The above practices to prevent empath pain are rewarding albeit the difficulty of mastering. Nevertheless, these practices have to be done for vampires and pain-inflicting persons to be thwarted away, giving them a much-needed message of warning that they cannot merely invade and inflict pain upon others (not just empaths).

In the case of geomantic empaths, they are experiencing pain because the earth is sick and in pain. This is not the earth attacking empaths in a psychic level. It just needs help in alleviating its own pain. Humans have the capability to transform these into positive energies before releasing it to humanity.

17

Understand Your Empathic Personality

There are two sides to the empathic gift that you possess. There is the positive, healing side of the gift and the negative, draining side of the gift. First, we will investigate the positive potential that this gift has and then, the struggles and dangers of it.

Positive Potential

The empathic gift has the potential to be one of the most critical assets humankind possesses: it can heal emotional wounds opened by tragedy, war, crime, and abuse.

There have always been diseases and conditions that even the most modern human medicine cannot cure. These diseases include such things as emotional problems as well as the sadness of losing a loved one to cancer, the horror of seeing one's home blown apart in war, the terror of having been a victim of rape, or the lingering trauma of having been abused as a child.

Empaths can relate to sufferers on a level that most people cannot. While empaths might not have experienced war, famine, crime, abuse, or any other tragedy themselves, they can feel on an intense and real level what it means to have experienced such things. Often, just having someone care and truly relate is what helps victims of these experiences heal.

Obviously, these experiences are the extremes of the tragedy and brokenness that plagues our world, but even in less extreme cases, such as a breakup, a fight between friends, the illness of a child, or the loss of a job, empaths are able to relate and help carry the burden of these things. The healing nature of the empath—the willingness to bear the burden of individual experiences and their emotional fallout—helps the world become a kinder place.

In addition, the empath has an incredible capacity for creativity and expression. Many times, your empathic gift will allow you to communicate what others cannot. A victim of war might have no idea how to express what the war was like, but in talking to the person, you come to have some idea and are able to write a poem, draw a picture, or express in some way what that experience was like. Empaths are like a bridge between those who are hurting and the rest of society. An empath takes the hurt that individuals are feeling and communicates it to the members of society chosen by the individual in a way that they can understand.

In other words, empaths are the key to a better society. They are the key to becoming more compassionate toward those who are broken-hearted for one reason or another. If you are an empath, your gift comes with a responsibility—a destiny, even—to change the world for the better.

At the same time, you must be aware of the struggles and dangers that you face as an empath. Let us look at these difficulties and discover how to steer clear of them.

Struggles and Dangers

There are three main areas in which empaths struggle: mental health, addictions, and relationships. We will take a look at each of these types of struggles in order to gain a better understanding of how your empathic gift can function (or malfunction).

Mental Health Issues

First, your empathic gift can be so overwhelming that your mental health suffers. You might even be diagnosed with bipolar disorder, borderline personality disorder, attention deficit disorder, generalized anxiety disorder, social anxiety, or agoraphobia. Although you may not actually have one of these disorders, it is not unusual for an empath to struggle with the same symptoms.

Wild mood swings are a telltale sign that you are an empath, but they can be mistaken for bipolar or borderline personality disorder. Depression is a common side effect of being an empath, since you absorb the emotions and energy around you and so much of the world's energy is negative.

It is also easy to be mistakenly diagnosed with attention deficit disorder, since your surroundings are so filled with stimuli that your mind cannot choose where to focus your attention. Your brain must process so many things are once, as you are not only processing your own reality but the realities of anyone around you, that you will seem disengaged with the outside world.

Anxiety is another common diagnosis for empaths. This diagnosis is prevalent because empaths are often very anxious about the negative energies they are receiving. You might become anxious in a crowd, for example, because you are overstimulated. You are receiving so much energy that it is unclear to your brain how you should handle it. This will make you anxious in that moment and memory will trigger a stress response the next time that you face a crowd. This can manifest as general anxiety, or more specifically as social anxiety, where interacting with others and absorbing their emotions causes you anxiety.

Finally, some empaths are diagnosed with agoraphobia. Agoraphobia is the fear of crowds and manifests often as the fear of leaving one's house. Many empaths have this fear, but it is not entirely unfounded. Leaving your home means interacting with people who likely have negative energy and who will likely steal your positive energy. Therefore, being afraid of leaving your house makes sense and is not just an issue of anxiety. However, agoraphobia is still debilitating to you as a person, hindering your participation in the normal functions of life.

Addictions

Addictions and bad habits are a common problem for empaths. You do not need to be ashamed if you have an addiction; this is simply your method of coping with an overload of emotions. Addictions may give you a sense of control that you do not have in your emotional life and seem to help in the short-term, but they will obviously cost you in the long run. Luckily, there are ways to overcome these addictions or more minor bad habits, which we will cover briefly in this part. However, this is just a brief overview of some common addictions, and should not be taken as medical advice. If you think you struggle with any addiction or mental health problem, you should consult a trained professional and licensed medical doctor.

First, you might have an eating disorder, whether it be overeating (binge-eating), eating too little (anorexia), or purging (bulimia). These kinds of addictive behaviors definitely fall in the category of giving you a sense of control. They can be very dangerous, and most often require professional help from doctors and therapists in order to break the cycle.

You might be addicted to some sort of substance, whether it be an illicit or prescription drug or alcohol. This often is a form of escapism—a way to avoid feeling the emotions and negative energies that have filtered into your mind, heart, and spirit. These are also very dangerous, and a professional will often need to intervene to provide you with accountability and support.

For mild unhealthy habits, like overeating junk food, or having a few glasses of wine each night, you can try to replace these habits with newer healthier ones. Things to remember in trying to break these negative habits: First, always replace a negative with a positive. Whenever you are cutting out a behavior or substance, you need to replace it with a positive habit or activity that you enjoy and that satisfies your craving. Second, you need to interrupt the pattern. If you know that whenever you are finished with work and you go home, your tendency is to drink alcohol, then change up your routine and go to the gym after work or go out with a friend. Third, try not to tempt yourself by having the substance to which you are prone to overuse close at hand, or try making the activity less accessible. This might mean not buying alcohol or junk food.

Whatever choices you make in trying to break your addictions or harmful habits, remember that ending your negative habits depends on the maintenance of your mental, emotional, and spiritual health. If you do not remain healthy in your mind, heart, and spirit, then your addiction could return any time you have a tough moment. This means that at the same time as you are working on breaking the addiction that you have, you need to improve your empathic abilities and skills to care for yourself in such a way as to become self-supporting and self-encouraging.

Relationships

Empaths often experience relationship problems and even enter toxic relationships. There are three types of toxic relationships into which empaths often fall: codependent relationships, abusive relationships, and parasitic relationships. Sometimes these relationship models overlap, so one relationship can fall into more than one category. Each one is dangerous in its own way and must be handled differently when trying to extract yourself.

The first type of relationship, the codependent relationship, is one in which you, the empath, define yourself by how you relate to another person so that outside that person's existence, you do not know who you are. You might be "Levi's mom" or "Nancy's husband" or "Richard's friend," but no matter by whom you define yourself, you do not know that you could go on without them. This goes beyond the normal fear of losing a loved one: you are absolutely terrified that, without them, you would have nothing.

The second type of relationship is the abusive relationship. In this type of relationship, the other person abuses you, the empath, using your willingness to take the blame for mistreatment. The abuser takes advantage of the abused in a physical, emotional, or sexual way, and the abused feels shame and guilt as though he or she is responsible for the abuse.

The last type of relationship is the parasitic relationship. This is a one-way relationship in which the parasitic individual takes advantage of the empath's listening ear and generous heart to get the empath to carry his or her burdens. Instead of asking the empath to share his or her emotional load, the individual shoves the entire burden onto the empath. The parasitic person never asks about the empath and never shows concern for him or her. Instead, in this type of relationship, the concern goes only one way. This puts the strain in the relationship on you, the empath.

18

The Healthy Empath

So, what does a healthy empath look like? With all this talk of the negative aspects of true empathy, it may seem like it truly is a curse. The good news is, an empath or intuitive who has learned how to create and maintain boundaries, and how to nourish themselves while filtering out the things that do them harm can live the fullest, richest lives of all.

Even those things might sound exhausting, like a full-time job. Rest assured, all it takes is some practice. Once you experience how good life can be as an empath, you'll begin naturally taking steps to thrive!

Meet Kara, a 36-year-old freelance writer from Brooklyn. She has been living in New York City for almost a decade. Kara has built up a client list that keeps her busy and comfortable in the apartment she shares with Rachel, a graphic designer she met through a mutual friend.

A typical day for Kara begins with making her bed, then ten minutes of yoga in her small bedroom, so that she can connect to her body and have some idea of what she's feeling physically and emotionally today. She then goes to their tiny kitchen and makes breakfast: oatmeal with chia seeds, because she has learned that that combination gives her energy but also fills her up. She doesn't have a gluten intolerance, but most glutinous foods tend to go straight to her brain and make her tired. She can't afford to nap all day long, so she has found out what foods sustain her and what foods should be reserved for special occasions when she doesn't have to work.

She'll make sure to drink a full 16 ounces of water with that, for the sole sake of hydrating well first thing. If she's not hydrated, she feels all sorts of aches and pains she usually wouldn't. She also takes a few supplements to help reduce inflammation and to regulate her physical energy levels throughout the day.

Kara makes sure that she takes breakfast either outside on their small balcony, when the weather permits, or at least beside the window because natural light soothes her. If it's raining in a good direction, she'll eat inside with the window partially open so that she can breathe in the petrichor—she's learned that the scent of rain fuels her creativity.

Then comes the coffee. A few months earlier, Kara began to have an energy crash mid-morning, sometimes so badly that she'd fall asleep while at the computer. She did some research and had to admit to herself that it was probably because her metabolism and adrenals were changing. She made the decision to switch to decaf, and within the first week noticed her energy stabilizing. While she still has the occasional caffeinated drink, she only brings home decaf coffees and teas.

While the coffee is brewing, Kara washes her dishes. A year ago, they realized that they had developed a bad habit of using too many dishes, then letting them pile up in the sink. It was taking too much time and energy to wash that many dishes, and it was also taking up a lot of precious real estate in their kitchen to have six plates, eight mugs (albeit cute mugs!), ten glasses, six bowls, seven small plates, et cetera. They downsized to one of each piece of table service a person and stored away the extra items for when they had company visiting. To make sure they could differentiate between what they were responsible for, they each selected recognizably different pieces. Kara's plates, bowl, and mug set were a faux copper, as were her utensils. Rachel's plates, bowl, and mug were Tiffany blue, her favorite color, and her utensils were pieces of real silver she'd picked up at Brooklyn Flea. Downsizing the kitchen in this very simple way had proven to be a fantastic way to save time and ease the frustrations that often came between them.

When the coffee is ready, Kara takes a few minutes to journal the things rattling around in her head. She may be a professional writer, but when you read her journal, you might not know that she is. It's not a beautiful prose to be cherished for generations, published posthumously. It's sentence fragments, and random thoughts untethered to one another by logic. It's all those things floating around, threatening to slow her down later in the day if she neglects them.

She takes another minute to enjoy her coffee, trying to see if anything else going on that she needs to pay attention to, but can't think of anything else that requires ink. As she finishes her coffee, she adds anything she needs to her daily to-do list and checks her calendar to be sure she remembers her appointment times for the day.

Then it's time to get ready. She'd showered the night before – something about going to bed clean always helps her get better rest – so this doesn't take long. Before leaving the house to meet her first subject of the day in Queens, Kara dabs a blend of essential oils onto her pulse points – partially for fragrance, partially for emotional grounding. She's going to be talking to victims of an arson today. She knows this has the potential to affect her, so she wants to be able to absorb the story but not carry the emotions with her all day.

Rachel has begun her morning routine, too. She tends to be more frenetic in the mornings, sleeping in longer and then rushing to get out of the apartment on time. At first, this was very jarring to Kara. She tried to be social, but the hurried manner and loud sounds that came from the whirlwind that was Rachel's routine irritated Kara. It took Kara a long time to attach the word irritating to her friend. She loved Rachel like a sister. Rachel worked hard and did her part in the chores. They had a fantastic time together when they were entertaining or out with friends, so calling a part of Rachel's persona irritating felt like a betrayal of some sort. But when Kara finally realized that it wasn't a slam on Rachel's character, and more about the way they gained and held and spent their energy, she was able to admit that yes, any rushed, loud action in the morning irritated her.

Understanding that busy mornings were a simple fact about Rachel, Kara decided it would be easier to change some of her own habits than to confront her friend. So, she began waking an hour and earlier in the mornings to be sure that she was back in her own bedroom, getting ready for work when Rachel became active. The occasions when Rachel has to be up early are the hardest for Kara, but she can manage those disruptions to her routine, as long as they're not the norm.

Life outside her apartment can't be as structured as her mornings. It's New York City, after all! Having to depend on others for transportation can be frustrating for anyone, and public transportation can fully drain a highly sensitive person. She's learned some coping skills over the years that are fairly standard for New Yorkers, like listening to music or audiobook, or reading when on the subway or bus, so she keeps a paperback and earbuds in her bag. She also knows that even in winter, she can overheat while waiting for a train in a subway tunnel, so she makes sure she has a bottle of water with her at all times.

Kara makes it to the café in Forest Hills with twenty minutes to spare. This gives her time to get settled and not have to rustle around in her bag or otherwise distract from the attention her contact deserves. When her contact arrives, Kara is able to focus on making her feel comfortable and asking questions without leading or presuppositions attached to them. She takes notes and, with her voice recorder running, she's able to get a story worth telling. By the time Kara pays the bill for them both, she ensures that the interviewee is pleased with how things went, and lets her know that if she thinks of anything else she wants to say, to contact her.

Checking the time, Kara sees that she should be able to get to her next appointment with almost an hour to spare, so packs up and heads to the subway station. Things are going well until she has to switch trains and finds out that one has a 7-minute delay. It's not a very big deal, but she feels anxiety creeping in. When the correct train comes, she boards. One stop into her ride, the train slows to a halt again. Over the loudspeaker, the conductor says something about the tracks.

Minutes pass.

She checks the time again—if they stay at this standstill much longer, she'll be late. She types a text to the client she's supposed to meet, but she doesn't get a signal. Twenty minutes later, the train begins to crawl. Some of her old habits of anxiety have begun to flare up, so she focuses on her breathing. This is a new potential client; she's concerned he'll think she's unreliable. Kara pulls out the rollerball of oils she uses to help soothe anxiety and applies them, and then pulls out her journal and jots down some of her fears. Finally, the train picks up speed, and eventually, she makes it to her stop. Topside, the text sends, and she receives two from her client, Darnell.

I left your name with security. They know where to direct you. Just come in through the Astor Place entrance.

Then, a few minutes before her text had sent:

We'd said 11:30, correct? I have to leave for a lunch meeting at 12:15. Please respond ASAP.

This is the sort of thing that used to send her into a small panic. She wanted to work with this company on the project, a narrative script for a promotional social media video. The pay was going to be better than she usually received, and she already had been working on several different angles. Most importantly, she felt as though tardiness said something about her character, which was something she protected. Kara moves out of the flow of traffic and takes a break to assess herself.

She realizes her shoulders are hunching forward and her neck is retreating into her clavicle —one of her telltale defensive positions. She works herself through a few breaths while still on the sidewalk and stretches her arms above her head and then clasps her hands behind her. This takes but a minute, but she feels more in control again. This is New York: public transportation delays happen. She'd left with ample time to get here, too, so it wasn't an issue of neglectful planning.

"He'll be reasonable," she said out loud. And if he wasn't, then it was possible that this job wasn't meant for her.

19

Four Types of Psychic Intuition

Now that we're discussing what your psychic intuition feels like and some signs that your powers are developing, let's take a look at the different types of psychic intuition and define them:

- Clairaudience

- Clairvoyance

- Clairsentience

- Clair cognizance

You may not have heard these terms before, so here is a brief description of each.

Clairaudience

is when it sounds like someone is speaking directly in your mind. Not in the same way as people with certain mental illnesses – this is more of a short answer to a question, or advice, and it shouldn't sound/feel harsh or discordant. The word "clair" means clear, and "audience" is from "audire" meaning to hear, so you are psychically "hearing" these messages, though usually, it is within the mind. It can sound similar to when you act out a conversation in your head, or similar to how you hear people talking in dreams. These sounds and messages can come from your spirit guides or from the spirit of someone in your life who has died.

Clairvoyance

is when you see images in your mind's eye that hold psychic significance. "Voyance" meaning vision, so clear vision. The next time an image springs into your mind, seemingly out of the blue, try to analyze it. It may have a symbolic (or very literal) meaning about something coming up in your life, or it may explain something you've been thinking or worrying about. Clairvoyance won't be a very specific flash into the future where you can see exactly an event that will happen as a movie in your mind – like how they show it on TV shows. It will be a subtle image or "vision" in your mind's eye. You may have had clairvoyant messages in the past without realizing it! Some examples of what is classified as a clairvoyant message could be colors, numbers or letters, words, pictures or images of people, objects, animals, places, or anything symbolic.

Clairsentience

(clear feeling) is probably the most common of the four. It is when you feel something is going to happen. If you've ever heard someone use the phrase "I can just feel it" or "this doesn't feel right" this is clairsentience. Clairsentience is often called your "gut feeling" or your instinct. Another aspect of clairsentience is being able to sense the emotions of others. Maybe you feel a wave of sadness before your friend walks into a room, and then they tell you their mother has passed away. Maybe you're on the phone with your friend who has a broken right leg, and you feel a brief pain in your right leg, even before knowing they broke it. Maybe you see your pet and suddenly burst into tears overwhelmed by sadness for no apparent reason, and within a week, your pet dies. These are examples of clairsentience.

Claircognizance

(clear knowing) is when your intuition helps you figure something out that your rational brain can't, something you're maybe stuck on. For example, if you're stuck in traffic, should you risk taking the upcoming exit to get out of it and take the backroad, or will that end up taking longer? You inexplicably decide to wait it out and soon traffic has cleared, and you're on your way. This is claircognizance. If you've ever heard someone say, "I just know" and they have no evidence to prove their certainty or no way of knowing but end up being right – that is claircognizance.

So how do you tell whether you're just having an ordinary thought or whether it's a psychic message? The messages and premonitions can often be quite subtle, but the way to tell is if something (image, sound, feeling, certainty) just pops into your mind with absolutely no relation to what you were just thinking about. This is probably a psychic message and not a thought. Usually, these psychic messages are quite strong as well, not a little afterthought at the back of your mind. However, sometimes they are quieter communications, so with anything that comes into your mind seemingly unprovoked, it's always best to try and look at it closer and analyze it – it may have some psychic significance.

With these four channels of psychic communication, if you just take a deeper look at the next sound, image, feeling or thought that springs into your mind unbidden, you may find some relevant psychic meaning to it. The message(s) will help you gain information, receive communications from the spirit realm (spirit guides, passed on loved ones, etc.), or reveal premonitions or predictions to you, that your other five senses can't. You may already have read this list and honed in on one of the four that you feel more connected with or that you think one of them will definitely come more naturally than the others. Maybe you have used one or more of these in the past, whether you realized it at the time or not. Maybe you've already noticed that you have more of an ability for one than the others. That is likely the one you will be strongest at and the channel you will receive the clearest most powerful messages in, at least for now. I don't mean you can't practice with the other types and strengthening them. There are many psychics who, for example, started off naturally talented at clairvoyance and receiving clairvoyant messages, but as they practiced, they gradually became more powerful at, and mastered, clairsentience and that became their strongest intuitive channel. This is just one example, but it's to show that you're never stuck in just one situation or skillset with just one option! Although if you wish to keep the one you have a knack for as your strongest ability, then by all means. Remember, psychic ability is like a muscle!

Each psychic has a specific way in which their power and intuition manifests itself, and it's often related to who they are and what sort of person they are. Everyone, regardless of ability, has one of four psychic personalities. You are either a spiritual intuitive, a physical intuitive, an emotional intuitive, or a mental intuitive. So how do you find out which kind you are and fits your psychic abilities? Well, each one manifests itself differently, and there are certain traits associated with each type that you can look over to aid you in discovering which one you resonate with the most, and which one seems to be more you. There is no official test, but each psychic personality is defined in the following paragraphs – and hopefully, you can get a sense of which one fits for you.

Physical intuitive are the ones that have deep attachments to important objects, and usually, psychometry (sensing things via touching physical objects) comes naturally to them. They are the ones who are more likely to use objects like tarot cards, crystal balls, palm reading or tasseography (tea leaf reading) to determine things about a person or the future and perform psychic readings. They are very literally hands-on when it comes to sensing energy, relying on physical presence or moving their hands close to an object or person to get a sense of things. This makes them the ones most likely to be drawn to the art of psychic healing, or the ones that usually have a natural talent for the practice. They are often homebodies and love organizing their home, furniture, and decorations according to their interests. Their home isn't simply some space for them to eat and go to sleep at night – it is their temple and haven from the outside world, and it showcases a piece of who they are. They spend a solid amount of time at home and often have a lot of clutter and trinkets around the house. They also thoroughly enjoy spending time in nature and grounding themselves.

Mental intuitives are the analysts. They will think things over repeatedly, turning it over and over in their minds until they find an explanation for something until they yield a result. They always make sure they consider every little detail, checking and double checking. They don't ever want to miss anything, and they're not big risk takers, nor are they very spontaneous. Mental Intuitive are more likely to be clairvoyant or clairaudient and receive psychic messages via imagery or sound in their mind, as this is where they spend most of their time. They tend to "live in their head" so to speak and can go for hours on end with merely the company of their own thoughts, just thinking. They are going to need the most information and ask for the most detail when they sit down to do a reading for someone. They are the ones to logic their way through something – logic, reason, and rationality are what they live by. When working on something, whether it be a psychic related task or otherwise, they generally have a good ability to focus and stay focused on what they are doing. They also tend to have somewhat academic interests, although this isn't always the case.

20

Tips for Empathy and Highly Sensitive People to Protect and Manage Your Own Power

It is necessary for these highly-attuned individuals to learn how to protect themselves from the energetic and emotional baggage that other people dump on them, intentionally or not.

Being an Empath or a highly sensitive person is a gift which must be embraced and celebrated, but sometimes it is also a curse that adversely impacts the physical and emotional well-being. The key is learning how to manage your own energy and become more aware of your personal power and needs.

- Both should calm their emotions by practicing meditation, setting firm emotional boundaries, and utilizing mindfulness tools.

- Empaths work on the energetic level, so carrying a protective crystal, cleansing the etheric body with sage, or seeking other forms of energy healing is recommended.

- Moving away from the source of negative energy, situation or "energy vampire". Physical closeness increases the absorption of negativity.

- Practice guerilla meditation for five minutes when you encounter a sudden impact of physical or emotional distress due to negative energy in the surrounding. Find an empty room, a quiet spot, or a bathroom and calm yourself. Feed yourself with love and positivity before facing the world again.

- If you sense that you pick up someone's negative energy, immediately surrender to your breath to center yourself and connect with inner power. Exhale stress, inhale calmness to purify pain or fear. Visualize the negative emotion as gray fog and lift it up and away from your body, allowing bright and clear light to enter.

- Set healthy boundaries or limits to stressful people or situations. Spend less time or avoid them. Learn to say no.

Using Crystals for Healing

The healing properties of crystals have been tapped since ancient times to cure ailments and restore the energy of the chakras. With the aid of crystals, the chakras are able to remove energy blockages, allowing healing to set in.

The Healing Crystals

There are lots of healing stones that you can use to manifest your intentions and create what you want in this life. Crystals are physical and tangible forms that connect you to the Earth, letting you harness their powerful vibrations and energy to get the desires of your heart.

Wearing or having intention crystals close is beneficial because they continue to pick up on your own energy, amplifying the positive vibes that you are feeding your desire. When you place a crystal over a particular chakra in your body, your own energy transforms, moves, shifts, pulses, or vibrates in accordance with its signature energy and properties.

In the magical realm of higher energy and vibration, crystals will guide you during your personal spiritual journey. It will remind you of your earthly connection while working in the manifestation of your intention.

Steps to Use Crystals

The starting point is to make a well-thought, specific, and clear intention to tap the power of the crystals. To set the intention, ask yourself what matters to you. Why do you need to change or upgrade this certain aspect of your life? When and what do you want to achieve?

Next, make a powerful intention and allow your own energy to connect to the healing crystal. In a way, the intention becomes a large part of its energy.

The right crystal will help you receive healing faster, so take time to choose. When you already have it, you need to clean and program the stone. Give it a purpose by telling it what you need and what you want. Hold the crystal in your hand, then close your eyes, take deep breaths three times, pronounce your intention (aloud or inside your head), and thank it three times.

This Is One Example of Setting Healing Intention.

"I implore the highest vibration of light and love to connect with my higher self to remove all unwanted energy in my body and any past programming. I command this stone to hold my intention [insert your personal intention]."

Do not forget to say thank you (3x) to give emphasis that what you desire already exists in the universe.

Ways to Use the Healing Crystals

There is no right or wrong way to use them for healing. You just need to establish your own routine, follow it, and feed it with your positive belief.

- Wear it as jewelry or clothing accessory. Wearing a healing crystal close to your skin helps balance your energy field.

- Put it in your home or personal space to nourish your personal energy throughout the day. Placing crystals like rose quartz near you when you are in a tub brings healing energy.

- Place it in your bag, purse, or pocket to enhance your energy level.

- Place it over a specific part of your body. Laying the stone is the direct way to access its healing properties.

- Put it in your car or home. Healing stones are also protective stones. When you place a crystal in your car, it blocks negative energy that can cause accidents or break-ins.

- Meditate with crystal to enjoy its healing energy and receive life-changing insights.

- Create a crystal layout to gain and transmute its energy. This crystal grid is an old healing technique that gives a powerful healing effect.

- Move it around your body to remove negative energy from head to foot. You can use a crystal wand to do this type of healing. It helps you work on your auric field while practicing crystal healing.

- Sleep with crystal near you. Allow the healing crystal to work its magical properties while you are sleeping. It helps remove fear, doubt, and other negative energies of your mind and heart.

Choosing the Right Healing Crystal

A crystal healing guide helps you figure out the perfect crystal to use for your particular physical or emotional problem. However, using your intuition is the best guide. Some crystals choose you, drawing you into their energy level. If that happens, you can always program the crystal according to your own intention.

For Clearing

Clear or white crystals like Moonstone, Quartz, or Selenite are very absorbent. They clean and remove all kinds of energy from the body. Use any of them during meditation to calm your mind. After using, you must clean it to get rid of the accumulated energy that it absorbed.

Releasing

Orange crystals like Sunstone, Aragonite, and Copper effectively clear negative energy, clearing out room for healthy energy that will energize your body. These stones are great to use when you are feeling down or tired.

Energizing

Red crystals that energize are Ruby, Jasper, and Garnet. These crystals are very powerful and can invoke sudden surges of needed energy. They are the best stones to use when you need a quick pick-me-up.

Calming

Indigo-colored stones like Lapis Lazuli, Kyanite, and Azurite are calming stones. The soothing power of these gemstones or any other dark blue and indigo crystals is to help ease anxiety and fragile energy.

Allowing

The brown crystals like Tiger's Eye, Halite, and Petrified Wood are very grounding. These healing stones protect and show you the right way during your journey. They guide, protect, and clear the path. Use them when you want to make room for a new relationship, new job, or a new purpose.

Balancing

Green crystals like Emerald, Jade, and Malachite are known for their balancing properties which are vital to physical healing. Most often, the diseases of the body are caused by too much of something such as too much unhealthy bacteria or too much acid. Excess of anything makes you sick. The green stones balance and redirect the energy flow.

Aligning

Yellow crystals like Amber, Mookaite, and Sulfur reorganize the energy patterns. These healing stones are best to use when you are establishing a new habit or trying to stop an unhealthy habit.

Uplifting

Violet stones like Obsidian, Tourmaline, and Apache Tears are powerful healing crystals. They vibrate at extremely high frequency and can combine a warm and cool spectrum of colors, lifting you up to higher powers and induce a unique spiritual experience.

Loving

Pink crystals like Rose Quartz, Rhodonite, and Morganite vibrate loving, healing, and compassionate energy. They are best for drawing in romance, deflecting anger, and making you feel loved.

Protecting

Black stones like Obsidian, Apache Tears, and Tourmaline deflect everything. These strong and resilient crystals can repel all types of negative energy, driving them away from you.

Communicating

Blue crystals like Sapphire, Angelite, and Sodalite help in resolving issues of communication. Use them to find your truth or allow the revelation of truth.

21

Strategies to Be More Empathic

How to Increase Your Empathy?

Some researchers believe that empathy is partly intrinsic and could be somewhat learned behavior. If this is true, then there must be some new patterns in how to approach this. The following strategies are a good roadmap to increasing your empathy:

- Take on activities and new skills that are outside of your comfort zone

- Humility may be the doorway through which is born empathy

- Make changes. Get out of your usual environment

- Check your progress. Ask for outside influences to tell you what they see in you

- Notice what moves your heart, what moves your third eye

- Expand your horizons and find new ways to do this

- Question your prejudices and intolerances and try to adjust

- Talk to people you normally would not talk to

- Expand your inquisitiveness

- Ask new and different questions

- Always do things that are new, different, and better

If you are looking for ways to increase your empathic powers, you may actually be seeking a better and more efficient way to connect with those powers you already possess. This is a somewhat abstract premise, and will need a degree of focus however it will become easier with repeated use. Here, mindfulness comes into play. So, the more we are "in the moment," the easier it becomes to evaluate and identify other's intentions, and motivations. Do not allow the banter and turbulence of life to become distracting. This can obscure the truth in what you are picking up from others and make it increasingly difficult to assess the value and intention on their words.

That being said, empathy is not only useful, it is fundamental to building healthy communication and alliances, and creating the needed social and management proficiency in today's world. Empathy, as a tool, is an endurance mechanism of sorts, and can be kept active though individual intention, however, as an individual's power increases, empathy levels often drop so there is a great need for more focus on the continuity of your "active" empathy and an increased awareness of the presence and current status of one's own empathy.

How To Manage and Strengthen Your Empathy

To enhance your empathy, you must first clear your mind of errant noise and interference, and then use your intention to increase the continuity of your thoughts in the form of empathic energy.

- Mindfulness and individual meditation can be a great deal of help to assure that this becomes easier with repeated practice
- Focus on calming yourself both inside and out
- Develop emotional perception
- Use your curiosity to access the moment. Ask questions that will expand both yours and others "picture" of what is happening
- Use your listening and observational powers to help determine inner feelings and emotions of the moment
- Control or catch your judgmental senses. Transform your momentary impulses to correct or critique another person into kindness and a more cautious manner, and ask them if you may offer an opinion

Remember to set a block of time out each day to work on your empathy. See your empathic senses as a most valuable tool to be used for the good of others and of your own life and aspirations.

Learn to make accurate determinations of what you perceive to be happening when you interact with others. Be certain that what your senses are telling you, is the truth. We, as humans, all possess empathy. Do not allow yours to lay dormant. Use all of your senses all of the time. Choose to be present to life. Expand your empathy and embolden your relationships. This, in turn, will vastly enhance your administrative and managemental skills.

Our brains are wired to light up with empathy no matter what happens to us or what we are thinking. We all have something called "mirror neurons" which are something like an automatic sensing mechanism that dials in other people's emotions and other signals we get from them such as how they move or their facial expressions and much more.

Did you ever have an experience where you were walking down the aisle with your buggy in the super market and somebody was coming straight at you. You make eye contact and them both turn the same way, both attempting to get out of each-others way? This is mirror neurons in action. The situation was temporarily out of your subjective minds control and then when, as in this case, it appeared you were going to crash into one another, the intuitive and cognitive mind steps in and finds a logical way around the other person. Then, you both smile at one another because you both realize that what just happened was odd in a strange way.

Our mirror neurons allow us to "see though their eyes," as it were, and this is why for instance, when we see someone fall down and scrape their knee, we the emotion of pain and think about our knees. If you see an individual crossing the street and then jump out of the way of a bus, we feel the danger in just the same way they did in that moment.

During the times when we may be thinking about something mechanical on our car or perhaps a movie we may have watched the night before, this is being done in our subjective and cognitive brain and will not easily connect to our sense of empathy. Our minds in these instances are busy with something else.

If you wish to heighten you're your abilities to use your empathy, you must be mindful and not be daydreaming. Meditation will be of great help in this area. Clearing your mind and thinking about one thing, with intention, will help make your empathy a more controlled event.

Take some time for yourself and learn mindfulness. Feel your surroundings. If you are outdoors, feel the breeze, hear the sounds of nature, the birds, a barking dog a long way away. All of it. Be in your moment. All of this is integral to meditation. The absolute best and easiest way to increase your empathy is to begin by improving your meditation regimen and everything that goes with it. Meditation and empathy are deep seated brothers in the human makeup. When you do one, you will be working very closely with the other.

There are things that your can do that are a sort of "practice" for mindfulness and empathy. Asking yourself what it is that you are feeling would be a good example of one of them. In dealing with emotions, try to name each emotion you are experiencing as your feel it, in different settings, as you go through your day. Then, you will learn to be much more intentional in setting up your control mechanisms as these emotions relate to each different environment or meeting.

Is it possible that our sense of empathy can be in a state of flux? Is empathy hard wired into our makeup or is it something we can work on and enhance?

These are both great questions. The answers are yes and yes! Empathy is indeed a teachable and a learnable emotion. The ability to understand and have feelings and emotions in common with others is not inborn so it can diminish or increase within your mind. It can also be taught and some medical professionals are using this theory in their current practices in order to help those people who they feel would benefit from it.

A current affairs example of empathy in flux has been occurring for several years now in the USA. Striking evidence has revealed that the current mass uptick of the digital revolution is now underway. Adults have reported that they have been the recipient of increasing amounts of online abuse and intimidation and studies show a long period of decline of empathy as a direct result of this activity.

Also, college aged young adults have experienced an extreme drop in empathy for well over the last twenty years. Another area reported to have experienced a huge drop in the activity of empathy is in the wealthy sector of our society. It appears that the wealthier you are, the less empathic you become. Add to that, senior executives are highly likely to exhibit behavior fitting of a psychopath and have been reported to be absolutely lacking in empathy. Much more so than the average worker.

In the area of crime, of course there has never been a great deal of empathy at work and today, there is even less than that. Religious violence and constant overseas war fighting have all but removed the memory of any semblance of empathy leaving one to wonder, what is happening to the human race?

We must get back on track where empathy is regarded. A society without empathy will not survive. The existence of human empathy is all that is standing between the animal kingdom and humankind. Something needs to be done, and empaths, while being all but overlooked by the medical and psychological communities, would appear to be the key to unlocking the pathway to a harmonious and peaceful world community.

"See this through my eyes and you will understand what I am telling you!" Would be a great way for everyone to get started rebuilding their own sense of empathy. This is a very important part of our everyday lives. Without empathy, we are lost. With prime exception of deep-seated psychopaths, everyone is wired to manifest the benefits of human empathy. This means that we all have the ability to walk in the other persons shoes and then to understand their emotions and their point of views.

Why wouldn't we already be doing this each and every day of our lives? Well, it is highly probable that people just don't think about it or do not care. Apathy is growing and empathy is shrinking. As an individual, you must try and you must focus on it with intention or it will not happen. In effect, we all need to sit down and think about apathy and practice doing in in ourselves.

The next time you go out in public, look at the people who are close by. Make eye contact and talk to everyone who will respond with polite conversation. I would be willing to bet that all of us, upon one trip to the grocery store or running some sort of errand, would meet somebody who could just use a hand. From bags of groceries to stuck wheels on shopping carts to auto breakdowns. We all need a hand up sometimes and the next time it could be you who needs one.

I remember back in school when I was just a kid and was learning to drive for the first time, there was a saying in the lesson plan that I could never forget. It was, "Courtesy is contagious!" And it applies across the board and not only for driving "manners." Do you believe in karma? I do and if anyone is keeping score, it may be time to stock up on good deeds. If you can see us all on this small blue planet as one race, one species, you can feel a kinship with everyone everywhere and this is a very good concept.

22

Crystals for Empaths

Empaths are highly-sensitive individuals who are easily affected by the overwhelming emotions of other people. It doesn't matter whether it is a positive or negative emotion, empaths feel it deeply which can affect their own feelings. Unless they learn to process or understand that the sudden, intrusive emotions are not their own, empaths' well-being is compromised.

One effective way to ward off the tiring emotions that can affect the physical, mental, and emotional health of empaths is to use crystals.

Getting Familiar with Crystals

Crystals are special and unique gemstones or rocks that are popularly used for protection and spiritual healing. These precious stones come from the womb of Mother Earth and contain potent healing energy. Each of them possesses certain elements that aid in healing, emitting a specific vibration that represents their own distinctive signature.

Benefits of Crystals to Empaths

The right and beneficial crystals help them deflect negative energy, become more grounded, and balance the emotions.

- Provide daily psychic protection from the sudden attack of energy

- Cleanse the aura

- Filter excess energy

- Prevent accumulation of energetic junk

- Heal silently and deeply

- Help to resolve emotional or mental confusion

- Release extra baggage or past issues

- Give loving energy and support to the wearer or carrier

- Ease the energetic and emotional stress, letting your life the way you want

Black Tourmaline

It is considered as the most powerful crystal for empaths because of its ability to absorb negative energy and keep it inside. As an empath, you are most vulnerable to electromagnetic frequencies and also to the strong influence of people or object around you. The Black Tourmaline will shield you against them.

This crystal repels black energy and prevents any type of psychic attacks that threaten your energy field. It is a great grounding crystal that acts as a sponge that absorbs dark energies, helping you see the light during dark times. Use it to send unwanted energy into the Earth for transmutation and healing purposes. It can also be used to direct purposeful energy to a certain person.

Black Tourmaline aids to ease and release tension or stress. It boosts the functions of the heart, adrenal glands, and immune system. It can be used to cure joint pains and inflammation. Aside from healers, it is also popular among magicians, shamans, wizards, and witches.

Rose Quartz

This beautiful crystal protects, soothes, and heals the heart chakra. It also aids in lowering blood pressure, improves circulation, and releases anxiety. This gentle, empowering, and soothing quartz is very powerful. It helps you radiate love and compassion, influencing people to become more positive and hopeful.

Empaths should wear or carry rose quartz to push away the negative energies that come to them. It is especially beneficial when you need to deal with toxic people and situations. If you are single or in a romantic relationship, having this crystal with you can help you find someone or deepen the relationship.

It is an excellent stone for grounding, allowing you to release past issues, struggles, negative thoughts, and pains. It is the best stone for people who experienced emotional trauma. As a grounding crystal, the rose quartz provides security and stability. Use it to express your unconditional love to yourself and to Mother Earth.

Amethyst

It is a calming crystal that can instantly dispel the effects of overwhelming emotions, helping you feel better. It protects you from the evil eye, curses, and negative energies that surround you.

The Amethyst offers psychic protection as well as enhance your psychic ability and spiritual awareness. It activates the power of the higher chakras, sharpening and heightening your intuition.

It is also a powerful manifestation stone, helping you connect to your heart's desire and make your wishes come true. As a healing crystal, it enhances the functions of the sympathetic nervous system, relieves headaches, balances hormones, and eases neck tension.

Malachite

This stone helps empaths eliminate stagnant emotional energy and allow fresh beliefs to set in. If you want to remove accumulated emotions that come from stressful situations and daily pressure, malachite is the ideal crystal for you. It absorbs all the negative feelings that you are holding inside, relieving you from suffering and pain.

Malachite gives the wearer the confidence to reinstate the personal beliefs that will bring personal happiness and satisfaction. It strengthens the sense of compassion and self-love. Place it under the pillow when you sleep to attract sweet dreams.

Hematite

This stone strengthens the auric field of empaths, fending off negative energies and unwanted vibes. Meditate with hematite in your hands and create a protective shield around your body. Imagine your aura pulsating and keeping you safe from any kind of external energy.

Hematite is also known for its ability to soothe emotions and keep you centered. It has a higher power that assists you to find the answers to unresolved issues and questions. If you want to rekindle your passion in life, use this powerful stone. It also aids you when you want to avoid energy-draining people or Psychic Vampires.

This grounding stone is deeply attached to the energy of the Earth. It is called Bloodstone because it cleanses the blood and heart, improves circulation, and regulates menstrual flow. It is also a great stress reliever, helping the nervous system to calm. It also boosts financial support from family and friends.

Fluorite

This gorgeous crystal helps balance emotions, giving you clarity and stability when you feel confused. To gain the instant benefit, place the fluorite on top of your third chakra, which is located between your eyebrows. If you want to strengthen your intuitive powers, use the rainbow fluorite.

Fluorite is also a positivity stone. Its immense power protects your aura, calms the emotional and mental chaos, and removes the negative energies. It can effectively clear the low vibration, helping you study or think with better focus. Furthermore, this crystal soothes inflammation, heals the mucous membrane, and decreases cold symptoms.

Lepidolite

This powerful stone increases the power of other crystals when it is placed near them. It is a beneficial stone for empaths because it can ease the anxiety that commonly plagues them.

Lepidolite is an empowering crystal that promotes peace, love, luck, and restful sleep. It helps you discover your hidden strengths and potential, leading you to your destiny and purpose in life.

Black Obsidian

This volcanic stone has a fiery protective energy that wards off unwanted energy from penetrating your aura and personal space. It is a very powerful stone that also repairs the aura.

Black Obsidian is also called the mirror stone because of its enormous power to help you view the world in its deepest sense of being, revealing highly - reflective things to heal your body, mind, and spirit. It helps you understand yourself better, gain wisdom and knowledge, and relieves deep-seated emotional distress. Use this empowering stone as an anxiety reducer and stress reliever.

Healer's Gold

It is a strengthening crystal which is also called Apache Gold. It helps you strengthen the energetic boundaries, acting as a psychic protective shield against negative emotions and vibrations.

The Healer's Gold also enables you to release the trapped energies inside you, giving you a fresh start as well as setting clearer signals to people that matter in your life.

Aqua Aura

This quartz which is bonded with gold deflects harmful energies acts as strong psychic bulletproof protection for empaths. It can effectively relieve trapped energies and emotions.

Chrysanthemum Stone

It is a protective stone which is characterized by a flower-like pattern. Chrysanthemum Stone builds an auric filter wall that reduces the number of people who are trying to enter your personal energetic boundary. It also reduces the level of psychic sludge.

Kyanite

A Black Kyanite is a powerful stone in meditation and visualization technique. To achieve your purpose, you need to empower yourself by holding it in your hand, then sweep all over the body to cut unhealthy energetic ties. It realigns the energy field and activates all chakras.

This stone protects your personal energy from those who want to steal your positivity. Moreover, it forces you to see what or who is putting you down, releasing unwanted and excess energy that is not your own.

Kyanite is also considered a stone of emotion. It aids the mind to create new paths, providing supportive and soothing effects. This powerful stone deepens the meditation, encouraging the opening of channels that lead to the spirit realm and boosting psychic abilities. It cures headaches, eye pain, the tension in the brow, and throat pains.

Ouro Verde

It is a green crystal that emits olive green light, protecting you from overwhelming emotions and energies that are trying to enter your personal space.

Flame Aura

This crystal is also known as the Titanium Aura or Titanium Quartz because it is bonded to metals especially Titanium. It acts as a protective buffer that shields empaths from harmful energies in the environment. The negative energies are pulled down by Flame Aura into the Earth to allow the process of transmutation.

Lapis Lazuli

Empaths are constantly bombarded by the energies of people who want support and attention, resulting in the accumulation of tiring and excess emotions that affect their personal energy. Lapis Lazuli is another protective crystal that will help decipher the barrage of intuitive impressions that you receive and set clear boundaries.

It is considered the crystal of truth and often associated with royalty and luxury during ancient times. Lapis Lazuli is believed to bring wisdom, clear judgment, and good communication. Having this crystal with you during troublesome or confusing moment helps you focus and gets rid of unnecessary thoughts. It heals the vocal cord and throat.

Citrine

This money and wealth crystal positively influence your financial stability. Aside from this benefit, it promotes the power of telepathy when used by empaths for their own purpose.

This beautiful stone also helps to recall past life memories, letting you discard the painful ones to balance your emotions. Moreover, it regulates digestion, stimulates metabolism, eliminates nausea, and enhances nerve impulses.

Magnetite

This grounding crystal helps to balance and align your energies. It can balance the polarities within your personal electromagnetic field as well as release the psychic overload that affects your well-being.

23

Stages of Empaths

There's a significant difference between compassion, sympathy, and empathy. In recent years, there's been a lot of attention to the characteristic of empathy and the experience of an Empath. Sympathy is the feeling of sorrow for another person's suffering without feeling what another person is feeling and being affected by it as an energetic echo of the other's feelings. Sympathy is purely a mental awareness of another's feelings.

Empathy is primarily somatic: it's felt in the body as sensory input. Like all sensory input, it might be felt, heard, seen, smelled, tasted, and so on.

An Empath feels another's feelings by allowing the energetic signature of the other person's feelings to vibrate in their own body. These feelings may be emotional or physical.

Some people are more generally empathic and experience this most, or even all, of the time. Even people who are not typically empathic will experience empathy at some points in their lives.

Compassion is empathy combined with wisdom. I'll explain further on this later in the book.

The Naive Empath

Many natural empaths don't know they're empaths. I refer to such folks as "Naïve Empaths." If you're a Naïve Empath, you could experience sensitivity to other people's energetic vibrations without realizing what's happening. You might have intense reactions to the emotional or physical states of others without realizing that these feelings are not your own and didn't originate from you.

As a Naive Empath, you're hit with waves of emotion or physical sensation that don't seem relevant to the situation you're in. You misinterpret the experience and assume there's something wrong with you.

The conventional assumption in our culture is that feelings, whether emotional or physical, begin and end within the mind of each individual and can't be felt by anyone else.

We are all deeply and completely interconnected with each other and all things. We try to fit our experiences into commonly accepted explanations, but our culture's predominant philosophical orientation is inadequate to describe our interconnection. You assume all your feelings originate from within you.

It's standard to assume every unexplained shift in feelings is due to some mysterious problem or malady within you. If you experience a sudden wave of anger or sadness, for instance, you look for some reason for being sad or angry.

"I guess I'm angry about what my boss said yesterday," they might suppose; or, "I feel sad in this store. I guess I don't like shopping."

There are always plenty of "reasons" to feel angry or sad. If you're looking for a reason, you'll find one. You can waste a lot of time and energy drumming up "reasons" to explain bad feelings, when, in fact, those feelings might not even belong to you.

When talking to a friend, an Empath might notice pain in their foot right before the friend tells them about the bunion surgery they have scheduled. A Naive Empath, who is completely unconscious of what's going on, might not even notice the connection. Others might assume a coincidence.

Learning about energetic empathy and vibrational interconnectedness helps by giving context and a conceptual framework to make sense of your experiences. It's easier to release negative energy fields once you let go of misplaced self-judgement.

A lot of people are highly empathic and don't know it. Such folks automatically take on and absorb other people's emotions without realizing they're doing it. Currently, the standard 20th Century psychological paradigm, that your thoughts and feelings are, and can only be, generated from your own brain, is the "conventional wisdom" to which most people subscribe. There is a very useful aspect of that paradigm that I still endorse; saying "You are making me mad" is not the same as saying "I feel your anger."

Let's say you're feeling okay, just fine. You go to the mall and on your way home you notice you're feeling really depressed for no apparent reason.

You think, "Wow, I must have some sort of unconscious issue coming up and that's why I'm depressed!" It's possible that you picked up on some stranger's depressed feeling at the mall. Because you don't realize that happened, it won't even occur to you to just release it with the thought, "That's not mine!"

Instead, you might suppress it and feel inexplicably depressed or you try to "process" the feeling psychologically. You will try to associate it with something in your life that you are "depressed about". Many naïve, or unconscious, empaths walk around with other people's stuff for years and never figure out that those feeling don't even belong to them.

I am not saying that every feeling or emotion you have is one you picked up from someone else. You generate feelings of your own, too. But if you suddenly and inexplicably find yourself feeling anxious, depressed, or angry, it is a good idea to clear yourself of whatever does not belong to you before you assume that you have some suppressed issue.

I am also not saying that you are not responsible for the feelings you carry around. If you have let someone else's feelings attach to you, it is your responsibility to release them. It's your responsibility to figure out how to prevent taking on unwanted feelings in the future.

Often, unconscious empaths will begin to avoid crowds and events because they find they often feel awful after being around people. They might have anxiety about social settings because they have experienced feeling bad for no apparent reason after being around a lot of people.

Again, because we are operating in a predominantly psychological paradigm, you might decide you have a social phobia or some other neurosis. You might have decided to avoid being around other people just to avoid getting their negative feelings all over you.

The solution to this problem is not to hide out in some sanctuary for the rest of your life. The world has too much to offer, and you have too much to offer the world! Once you realize that you are an Empath, and that's why you are so inexplicably miserable, you can learn clearing and protective methods.

In most of Western society today, psychology is the predominant paradigm used to explain emotions and feelings. For the most part, psychology tells us that if we are feeling depressed and anxious for no apparent reason, it can only be caused by one of two things: suppressed subconscious issues, or a biological, chemical imbalance.

I agree that chemical imbalances are real, and some people are benefited by use of medications to manage emotions better. Chemicals are vibrations just like everything else in the universe. Therefore, it's possible that introducing chemicals into our bodies may help bolster deficiencies and suppress excesses. This isn't fundamentally any different than vitamins or other supplements. I also agree that we're affected by subconscious material that influences how we feel. However, there is a third cause of inexplicable feelings of sadness and anxiety that "seem to come out of nowhere".

The third cause is that some people take into themselves the feelings of other people. If you have no frame of reference to understand what has happened, you naturally assume you have some sort of unresolved issue you just can't lay your finger on.

The Novice Empath

Some empaths are newly aware of their empathic gifts and how their sensitivities affect them but haven't learned to manage the experience; I call folks at this stage of development, "Novice Empaths." If you're a Novice Empath, you might feel vulnerable to every negative energy field or person you encounter. You might even feel like a helpless victim of other people's pain.

"I can't go where there's too much negativity," you tell yourself.

"I'm getting attacked by negativity," you say, feeling trapped and unable to move freely through the world.

Empathy has an important role to play in the collective evolution of human consciousness. It won't do to have all the empaths curled up in the back of their closets, waiting for the world to be less negative.

By shifting your awareness, learning mindful detachment, plus a few other helpful energy-shifting methods, you can effectively interact with the flow of empathic information you receive.

If you are too strongly impacted by others, it's because you are subconsciously grabbing hold, and refusing to let go, of the energetic vibration you're picking up. This occurs either because of a lack of awareness of the nature of the experience, as in the Naïve Empath, or a lack of skill, as in the Novice Empath.

When you experience something that many people don't understand, you might think one of these things about yourself:

"I'm weird."

"I'm special."

Naïve Empaths frequently adopt the position, "I'm weird." The Novice Empath is prone to think, "I'm special."

Believing you are "special" or believing you are "weird" are two sides of the same coin. In either scenario, your ego attaches to the experience, grabs hold of it, identifies with it, and believes, "This is me."

Here's a good definition of "attachment." Attachment is confusing experience with identity. Even feelings that originate from within you, and your experience, are just passing through. You can feel what there is to feel, and gain the useful information that's available, and do it without grabbing hold and getting attached.

The Empath's experience is real. It isn't at all far-fetched that sensitive people can feel energy. It's more natural to feel energy than not to feel it. In order to be numb to energy fields, you have to exert unconscious effort to numb out and not sense what is all around you.

Here are some thoughts that might plague a Novice Empath:

"I'm an Empath, so I have no choice but to feel this."

"I'm an Empath, so I have to be careful what I expose myself to."

Or "I could shut myself off to feeling, but I'd miss feeling all that I do. So, I just have to accept feeling bad."

If you are staying sick, depressed, or angry by feeling the feelings of others, it's not because you have to. It's because you're grabbing hold of these sensations and refusing to let them pass through. You are identifying with the feelings, and the specialness, of being an Empath.

Here's a method for letting go of trapped energetic patterns:

1. Notice the sensation.

2. Acknowledge that it's not "weird" or "special." It's just one of the possibilities of the human experience. (This will help you avoid attaching.)

3. Allow yourself to gather any helpful information about the person or situation you're sensing.

4.   Recognize that these sensations don't belong to you, and you don't need to hold them.

5.   Be aware of any Ego chatter about how you are "taking away their pain" because "you can handle it better" than they can. (This is a classic martyr complex. While on the surface it may seem noble and generous, it's disrespectful of the other person's power and autonomy.)

You are a marvelous cell in the marvelous Great Mind. As you develop, you advance the development of The Great Mind of which you are a part. You're an amazing participant within an amazing universe. However, you'll save yourself some time if you don't confuse this with being "special."

So, what's so bad about feeling special? It isn't bad, but it's a trap. The concept of specialness is tied energetically to the concept of separateness. Separateness is an illusion and is one of those things that make the ego extra sticky.

Ideas of separateness, and the hierarchies that inevitably arise from such ideas, are an illusion. Your ego never tires of categorizing and labeling you and all of creation. It builds hierarchies and opinions about everything, in an attempt to stay "safe" from the "unknown". The ego is going to do this. No need to fight it. Just don't fall for it.

24

The Empathy Coping Mechanism

If you feel through reading this book that you identify as an empath, then congratulations! You have taken the first step forward into healing and taking back your power. The following part is going to offer ways in which you can learn to filter, channel, understand, respond, and relax for yourself so that you can not only survive as an empath but also thrive as a powerful individual.

Every person interprets and integrates to the world differently—yours just happens to be a highly sensitive one. You have taken this huge step in realizing that this is how you absorb information and have probably been suffering for it, repressing it, and constantly feeling guilty for your sensitivity. However, you no longer have to feel this way, as there are many ways that you can learn to cope with your nature and use it as a tool to follow your dreams, make the world a better place, and ultimately, heal yourself.

Coping Mechanisms

Before you go out and try to heal the world and achieve your dreams, you need to adapt to certain coping mechanisms that will help you through the tougher moments of your sensitivity. For this part, you might want to have an empty notebook ready, as writing things down makes it easier to commit habits to memory before you commit them to bodily memory. Here is a list of the habits you can apply to your life that will help you nurture your inner universe when the outer universe begins to feel like too much:

1. Identify: First and foremost, you need to learn to identify the things that you personally as an empath find the most draining to your energy, and also, the things that exist to energize you. Make a list in your notebook of these things in two separate columns. If you aren't entirely sure, bring this notebook around with you so you can identify these drainers and energizers at the moment. Try also to write down what you feel mentally and physically as you are being drained/energized. By doing this, you will know which environments zap you faster of energy than others, such as a mall or interacting with a certain person, and then you can learn to limit it. At the same time, you can balance these zapping situations with environments and activates that replenish this energy. Do this for an about a week and notice how you are feeling.

2. Create a Shield: There are some situations that you cannot avoid, even if they drain you, such as family functions, work functions, and other social events, even certain people. An energy shield is a way for you to cope while you are within these situations; this requires great effort and practice on your part. What it does is that it essentially lets in what you wish to let in, but also deflects anything negative away from you. Think of a bubble surrounding you—most people usually think of a bubble of light. Within this bubble is your world, and you choose what comes in, and what comes out. If you feel your energy is being drained in a certain situation, you can retreat into this bubble and find yourself feeling safe, while everything else and everyone else is outside. This all comes down to awareness and noticing what you are feeling and how fast your energy is being drained.

3. Observe Your Thoughts: Depending on whether or not you have certain mental health disorders, it may be hard for you to create a shield to prevent negative thoughts and feelings from coming into your mind. The next best approach is to watch over your mind and learn to identify their source. For example, if you feel angry, and are having angry thoughts, try to identify if this is coming from someone else or from you. Once you have figured that out, it will make it easier to find a solution to your anger, since you are no longer confused about where it comes from.

4.   Positive Affirmations: It may be helpful to you to have a handful of positive affirmations nearby, such as on your phone or written down, to help you should any negative thoughts or mood come about. You can identify if these feelings are yours are not, and if they are not, you can say your affirmation to return yourself back to the present moment.

5.   Grounding: You may feel a stronger connection toward the universe and the earth as an empath than to those around you. If this is true, you can learn to take any negative energy and feelings you may have absorbed and redirect them into the Earth, where they are absorbed and dealt with. This can help you strengthen the bond between you and the Earth as well, should you feel a distinct connection.

6.   Forgive: Forgiveness is the emotional process of releasing negative energy and letting it go on its way. Forgiveness can be difficult for empaths, as they are often the victim of being used for their kind, understanding nature. This is also why forgiveness is especially important for empaths too; holding onto hate or anger will drain you more than the average person. Detaching from this negativity will help you on your venture toward healing. Forgiveness can also be applied to yourself; for things you may have done to others, or for the hurt you allowed others to give you.

7. Catharsis: Empaths often have difficulty processing the emotions of others that they forget to process their own. They inadvertently allow their own emotions to build up, allowing them to affect their inner world negatively. Participating in catharsis is when you allow yourself to feel the emotions at their most potent, whether it be laughing, crying, yelling, etc. They are ways in which emotions are expressed, and are also the outlets to allow this pent-up energy to be free. Try to find a way to let your emotions out in a moment that feels right and appropriate for you.

8. Make a "You" Time: Self-care has shown to be one of the most important ways a person can cultivate their own mental health in a positive manner. Making a "you" time is similar—it is time to take care of yourself, that not everyone is always going to understand. If they really care about you, then they will realize that you are doing this for your own well-being. Try to set aside at least two evenings a week where you can apply some of the previously listed skills to practice, or at least an hour before bed should two nights a week be difficult for you. Remember, that you do need to prioritize yourself as an empath, as this is the only way that you are going to heal and begin taking your power back.

9.   Create a Safe Place: It is going to be a lot easier to replenish your energy in a place that helps you relax and is comfortable. Try to make a space that is solely for relaxation purposes. It can be anywhere, but it's best for you not to do anything else while you are choosing to recuperate—like watch TV, organize your life, make phone calls—this will only distract from the recovery process.

10. Eating Well: Highly sensitive people are far more in touch with what is put into their bodies. If they don't eat well, they won't feel well. So of course, it would make sense for you as an empath to try to maintain a healthy diet of fruits and vegetables, meats, and some treats in moderation. It is common for empaths to want to binge on snacks or foods that aren't healthy in order to nun their oversensitivity, so pay attention to this should you feel it applies to you. Keep a diet journal and coordinate your feelings with what you ate that day.

11. Meditation and Yoga: This is all a part of the self-care era that has flourished in popularity within the Western culture as of late. It has for a reason though, and can greatly benefit those who are very sensitive like you.

12.   Get into Nature: Walking around outside and in nature has been proven to be one of the most effective ways to replenish the energy of an empath. Nature is full of vibrant energy that you can soak in, plus, it allows you to be on your own and reflect on your thoughts, life, and better ways you can apply self-care in your life. The still allows you to feel your own emotions, instead of everyone else's all the time.

13.   Alter Your Perspective: Because you are an empath, being kind and caring to others comes naturally to you. It is odd when people behave in selfish ways, and it tends to bother you greatly. Because this bothers you so much, it might help you to view them as people who are hurting, rather than people who are evil. They were raised differently than you, or have gone through some trauma that has made them feel this way about the world around them. By seeing them in this light, you can lessen the effect they have on you because you are choosing to understand rather than indulge in confusion and annoyance.

14.   Cleanse Your Chakras: Another new-age notion that has been popularized in the Western World is the concept of cleansing your chakras through meditation and yoga. The chakra system is specific areas of the body that run along the spine that supposedly contain energy and are paramount spiritual areas that you, as an empath, should

focus on. Beyond doing yoga and participating in meditation, many people apply aromatherapy or use crystals to absorb the negative energy that clogs up your chakras. Look up meditations on YouTube and begin to learn more about what these chakras mean in accordance with your empathic abilities.

15. Gratitude: The power of gratitude has been constantly documented within the confines of the meditational world, as well as many methods of enhancing wellness. Living life as an empath may often feel like a burden, and you may have felt angrier rather than thankful for possessing this sensitivity in your personality. But if you try to look at it from a different angle, you can see the enhanced ability to experience life to the fullest that other people often cannot attain until they are much older. You feel things deeply, which means you are going to see the glory of life much keener than a friend, while at the same time, you are going to feel the sadness of the world much more intensely too. Life comes with both aspects of existence, and your ability to feel them will allow you to learn more life lessons and become closer to people much quicker than others. Being thankful for this ability is one of the ways that you can shift your perspective on yourself, and also sends out positive energy into the universe that can make you feel calm rather than dismayed.

16. Set Boundaries: This is one of the most important skills that you must learn to develop as an empath. Not everyone is a toxic monster who consciously wants to take advantage of you—some people are simply adjusted to your caring nature and use you in ways that they do not always realize. Setting boundaries is an act that everyone needs to implement into their lives, the extent dependent upon how giving and unassertive their nature may be. Some people are more aggressive in nature and believe that this is being assertive.

17.

25

Connecting with Spirit Guides

One aspect of meditation and spiritual work that we've touched on has been Spirit Guides or Guardian Angels. Spirit Guides are another invaluable tool for the psychic, whether you want to meditate to simply ground yourself and replenish your energy, draw more strength to yourself before you begin a reading, or whether you seek help/protection – these are all reasons to attempt to connect with your spirit guides and ask them for advice and strength. Always treat them with respect when making requests or asking something of them. Do not demand things from them, but do not be afraid or ashamed to ask for help, as we can't do everything alone. Treat them as you would a friend or mentor.

Spirit guides or guardian angels – whichever name you use the term is clear – are not deities that you must worship; they are a spiritual presence that watches over you and guides you. You do not need to fear some godly wrath – they are on your side and want the best for you!

There are a few different types of spirit guide. Your guide may take the form of an ancestor or loved one who has passed on from the physical realm but continues to watch over you. If they are an ancestor, they may be someone who died before you were born but there are certain signs that crop up that a relative who knew them will tell you means their presence is near – for example, if you had a grandmother who loved flowers, and flowers are a constant presence in your life, this may be a sign that this ancestor is watching over you. Ancestral Guides can go back many generations. You may not see the face of your ancient ancestor when connecting with them, but you will sense their relation and connection to you. You could also be watched over by a dear loved one who died during your life. This would most likely be someone who died earlier in your life as spirit guides tend to watch over you for your whole life, but it could be someone who passed on later as well.

Another common type of spirit guide are the ones that come in the form of animals. These are called 'animal guides. You will likely be guided throughout your life by multiple different animal guides, each having something different to show or teach you – you won't just have one animal spirit that's assigned to you. Animal guides are often considered symbolic, or energies that embody the spirit of whichever animal it is that represents them. If you see a vision of a fierce panther while meditating, this Spirit Guide may offer protection and advice on assertiveness. If you see a bull calmly standing in a field, it may be there to help steady you.

Your spirit guide may not be ancestor nor show itself as any symbolic representation. It may just be pure energy, often seen as a brilliant light. This is what many people refer to as an angel. It is likely a comforting and familiar energetic entity that has watched over you since your conception. Make sure any entity you are connecting with truly is your spirit guide. If there is any feeling of darkness or discomfort, then that entity is not your spirit guide. Your only experience with your guide/s should be positive – that's how you know for sure.

Now that you know the basics of what a spirit guide is, let's look at how we can reach out and contact/communicate with our guides. This may be your first time interacting with your guide – you may not even know what form your guide will take yet!

Meditation is most people's go-to way to contact their spirit guide. There are many guided meditations available online for contacting your spirit guide. If you're not doing a guided meditation, when you sit down to meditate, make your only focus contacting your spirit guide. If you are contacting them for a reason, you can also focus on the reason you wish to communicate with them, but at the beginning, just focus your purpose on meeting your spirit guide. Clear your mind and don't force anything. Like with every aspect of spirituality, don't be frustrated if it doesn't work right away. Just keep sitting down to meditate with the powerful intention of contacting your spirit guide. They may not appear to you in a vision or as an image, but if you keep your mind clear and let it flow naturally, you will begin to sense their presence, and over time your communication channel with them will become stronger.

You can contact your spirit guide through meditation, but sometimes they will show themselves to you without you being in a meditative state or reaching out to them, such as a crow swooping down to stand directly in the middle of the path you were walking down, eyes fixed on you, or your grandmother's scent suddenly filling your nostrils for a moment or hearing a song that you always associated with your uncle who passed away. These could all be the presence of your spirit guide.

Certain times, when your intuition strongly urges you to do or not do something, so clear it almost sounds like an inner voice is speaking to you (similar to clairaudience), this could be your Guardian Angel, giving advice or warnings in your day-to-day waking life. You don't have to do anything to experience this communication; just listen and acknowledge the advice. Your guide, in the spirit realm, likely knows things that you don't and has wisdom you may not, so it's always a good idea to trust them – but at the end of the day, it's your decision to make. They are guides, not dictators.

Your spirit guide/s may visit you and show themselves to you in the form of a dream. If you've ever had a particularly vivid dream where a benign entity (whether your dead grandmother, an animal, or an energetic presence) has spoken to you, signaled to you, or led you to something/somewhere, and you remember it clearly the next day, or at least you remember the essence of what they were communicating and showing to you, this was likely a visit from a spirit guide. Though you may remember the figures you encountered and what was communicated to you when you wake up, you are likely to forget important details – if not your whole dream as the day goes by –, so it's a good idea to keep a dream journal and write down exactly what you dreamed about in as much detail as you can remember after waking up. If you have to rush out the door to work, you can write in the notepad on your phone – it doesn't need to be anything fancy. If you want to keep a record of spirit guide encounters, symbolic, and important dreams, you can copy it into a paper journal when you get a chance. If you want to plan to meet a spirit guide during your dream, focus on a question you want answering or the reason you wish to contact them before you go to sleep. As you drift into sleep with this in mind as your focus, hopefully, you will encounter them in your dream that night. This is a system of lucid dreaming, so keep in mind that it may take a few tries to have this sort of control over your dreams.

No matter what form your spirit guide takes, and what purpose they're there for, it's possible to create a strong connection and channel of communication with them through practice. Remember: if an entity that you think is your spirit guide makes you feel negatively in any way or is surrounded by any dark or unpleasant energy, that is NOT your spirit guide, and you should disconnect from them. Your interactions with spirit guides should always be positive – if somewhat introspective, or if they're a dead loved one's spirit, then possibly bittersweet. Your spirit guide and guardian angel only wants the best for you, and they can be a great source of support that you shouldn't hesitate to draw on.

Conclusion

It should have been informative and provided you with all of the tools you need to achieve your goals – whatever they may be. Each moment you spend out there, you are unsure of what emotion you will feel next. Frustration, excitement, grief, anxiety, joy, angst, annoyance, you name it. Thanks to your introspective mind, you have found out that you only feel these emotions when you are surrounded by people. And it's precisely why you have developed a tendency of running away from them every time you get overwhelmed.

The next step is to go forth and start utilizing the tips, tricks, tools, and techniques provided in this book to begin realizing your psychic potential and to become confident and empowered as your journey into the world of psychic power progresses. As you become more confident in your abilities and begin to see more results, you will have the desire to attempt some of the more difficult techniques and psychic reading styles suggested and described in this book, such as telepathy, crystal ball scrying, mediumship, and aura reading. And remember: it's true what they say – practice really does make perfect! Hence, if something doesn't work for you right away, it doesn't mean that it won't work or that you cannot use that technique!

An empath is a person with the special gift of picking up on the energies of the people around them and believing them to be their own. These are the categories of empaths:

- Emotion empaths: They pick up on the emotions of other people and believe them to be their own. If they stay near sad people, they end up becoming sad, and if they stay near happy people, they end up feeling happy.

- Medical empaths: They can detect the physical status of other people's bodies. They can tell what's ailing a particular person in an instant.

- Geomantic empaths: They are attuned to certain environments or landscapes.

- Plant empaths: They share a connection with plant life. They can intuitively communicate with various plants.

- Animal empaths: They share a strong connection with animals. Animals trust them, and they can sense their feelings.

- Intuitive empaths: They can pick up information from people by paying heed to their gut feeling.

- Psychometric empaths: They can pick up the energy from various objects.

- Precognitive empaths: They are aware of future events long before they take place.

Everyone can use any of the tools mentioned in this book – though, for some, it comes easier than for others. If you see someone who has started a beginner like you but are now better at using a certain practice, it may just come more naturally to them. Don't judge yourself and your progress based on others – just stick with it, and you'll see how far you progress. Moreover, there are likely to be things that come more naturally to you than to others, so don't worry – it evens out!